Impressive •⁄•

PRINTMAKING, LETTERPRESS AND GRAPHIC DESIGN

gestalten

Ink Different •⁄•

A little over two decades ago, Alan Kitching's Typography Workshop "breathed life into the dying embers of letterpress," according to British graphic designer Derek Birdsall. While the craft itself never went away, old-fashioned printing techniques have enjoyed a quiet resurgence of late, accompanied by the rediscovery and appreciation of crisp fonts, stylistic flourishes, and sharp page impressions, as well as the substance and substrate below: the singular, tactile – and often unpredictable – qualities of different inks, paper types, and binding techniques.

Inspired by the exhilarating and frustrating joy of the challenge, of hands-on tweaks and hit-and-miss results, modern digital nomads from all realms of the creative spectrum have started to re-explore the crafts of their grandfathers to "feel more rooted and less like a fraud. It's simply great to be able to say: look, I did this with my very own hands!" (Hendrik Weber/Pantha du Prince).

Driven not by a Marxist spirit, but by the sheer joy of experimentation, of old-fashioned tinkering, of "blood, sweat and smears," and of the thrill of the final product, more and more graphic designers, illustrators, and typographers have started to scour abandoned print shops, attics, and yard sales for outdated mechanical marvels – to give them a loving new lease of life and control their own means of production. There is a huge satisfaction in following through from beginning to end, from first flight of fancy to the finished card, print, or book, and – quite literally – leaving your mark on a piece of paper, a tangible imprint on the imprint.

While many of the artists in this book explore the joys and vagaries of letterpress printing, others have turned to hand-cut linotype, finely chiselled woodblocks, limited screen-prints, or embossing techniques. Yet, no matter what the chosen medium, the result translates equally well to the creamy crest of a formal invite or the slashed lines of a punk rock poster.

⋯> STOP PRESS

Incidentally, little has changed in letterpress printing since Gutenberg's movable type took over from traditional woodblock printing in the 15th century: Then and today, a reversed, raised surface is inked and pressed onto a sheet of paper, and only the level of automation may vary. Limited to the juxtaposition of pre-existing elements – of a few fonts, sizes, and extraneous borders and flourishes – letterpress was the original "out of the box" solution: It provided a set of building blocks for any occasion, whether wedding, funeral, or upcoming elections.

Restrained by line-width and colour options, typesetters would focus on bold head-lines, dates and statements, using serifs for added legibility, and frame them with a few ornamental details or brackets. "The old guys got it remarkably right – there was an intuitive understanding of what constituted readable text." (John Kristensen, Firefly Press).

Largely displaced by cheaper and more versatile offset printing in the second half of the 20th century, letterpress was (re-)popularised in the 1990s by mainstream home improvement guru Martha Stewart, of all people, who espoused its beauty for wedding invitations. Nowadays, the boutique printing scene or "Small Press Movement" covers the entire gamut of typography, illustration, and graphic design, from art monographs and limited edition publications to on-demand designs and corporate stationery.

⋯> NEVER OUT OF SORTS

Letterpress can be an unforgiving medium, yet it offers a three-dimensional quality unrivalled by other printing method – the physical bite into the paper adds its own topography, hills, and troughs, and definition to crisp lines, patterns, and typography. Here, styles and technologies go hand in hand: while limited line-width or color options force new approaches, the cheeky pleasures of overprinting, of deliberate mistakes, of smudges, splashes, and splurges, add a personal signature to the finished product. Akin to early mechanical typewriters, type itself becomes a finger print, a true identifier and subtle signature, visible only to those in the know.

Functional and bold, yet very expressive, Wild West saloon posters are a prime example of 19th century letterpress aesthetics. Incidentally, a lot of the medium's current pioneers hail from the American Midwest, from the backwaters of it's former frontier towns. Crafty – and craft-oriented – they espouse the nation's rediscovered maker spirit, a self-reliant go-getter attitude combined with an irresistible urge for tinkering.

Attracted by the engineering aspect, by intricate gears and levers running on ingenuity and elbow grease, they delight in the precise movements of arms and plates, the smell of ink and oil, the pre-steampunk wunderkammer appeal of their restored mechanical helpers. The strong reliance of human input and ingenuity is reflected in the medium's terminology – a press has jaws, knees, and elbows, pages are held by furniture, and a single character is known as a sort – if you run low, you are "out of sorts".

So, whether hand-cranked or automated, the labour-intensive process might take a week or two from start to finish: color is picked, mixed and applied by eye, not catalogue number, sheets are frequently fed by hand, and individual hues require separate runs. "I guess a skilled printer could run off 2,000 copies an hour – but we have never been in that much of a hurry." (Kristensen)

⋯> LEAVING AN IMPRESSION

In the current climate of corner-store calling cards and exchangeable software templates, these tangible human touches and skills – with all their idiosyncratic errors – have become a rare luxury. Sumptuous, luscious, almost prohibitively elaborate and sinful, bespoke hand-crafted cards and invitations reconnect sender and recipient as a thoughtful reminder and promise of things to come. Translated to the corporate sphere, to tailored company stationery or annual reports, hand-printing adds that certain je ne sais quoi, a dash of instant kudos and character. Limited by design, it conveys appreciation for the recipient and certainly leaves an impression – on the card stock and in our minds.

⋯> BEYOND STATIONERY

Blooming and blossoming in the niche, it was the relatively recent resurgence of DIY and maker culture, and its associated internet platforms and knowledge networks, that helped to make this type of small-scale bespoke printing commercially viable. All of a sudden, bedroom nerds and flamboyant artists alike found themselves with an internationally scattered, yet sizeable audience for their hand-cranked craft. After all, a one-man cottage industry might only need a few small-scale commissions and recommendations to stay in business.

And this expansion from coast to coast, from poster to coaster, has also broadened the aesthetic scope of today's DIY designer-printers. Working from and with their chosen medium's given quirks and limitations, many make a beeline to the not-so-distant past, to the early and mid 20th century and nostalgia-infused naivety, to post-war optimism, geometric exercises in modernism, or – even further back in time – Victorian filigree flourishes and frontier fonts. Others translate the characteristics and limitations of letterpress, screen-printing, woodcuts or linotype to the latest contemporary illustrations.

Among the cute, quirky and downright amazing creations assembled in this publication, we come across further paper manipulation and enrichment techniques, street-art-to-art-print silkscreen creations, landscaped linocut takes on nature, fish-scales as a printing matrix, hand-whittled stamps and even yogurt-infused pancake portraits – now with added sprinkles.

And this spirit of reclaiming the "means of production", of taking control of the printing process, also extends to the product itself. United in their unbridled love and attention to detail – visible or otherwise – even the more elaborate works exude an egalitarian spirit. This is art and craft for everyone – unique, precious and affordable.

Dolce ⟿

CHICAGO WEDDING · 2009 · INVITATION *(top)*
CLIENT Elizabeth & Steven PRINTER Dolce Press PRINTING Letterpress - Heidelberg Windmill 10x15

SAND DOLLAR WEDDING INVITATION · 2009 · INVITATION *(upper left)*
CLIENT Michelle & Thomas PRINTER Dolce Press PRINTING Letterpress - 8x12 Chandler & Price Old Style
Invitation is letterpress printed and combined with other flat-printed pieces such as an antique map, directions/travel information, registry card. All of the pieces are combined in a kraft stock box packed with beach grass. The box is closed with a wide blue ribbon and custom sticker.

KRAFT STOCK BUSINESS CARDS · 2009 · BUSINESS CARD *(left)*
CLIENT Stu Horvath PRINTER Dolce Press PRINTING Letterpress - 8x12 Chandler & Price Old Style
The cards were printed on kraft coaster stock in black, double-sided. The edges of the cards were painted with a black ink to match the front and back.

PHILOMATH PENGUIN BUSINESS CARDS · 2009 · BUSINESS CARD *(bottom)*
CLIENT Jacob Pierce PRINTER Dolce Press PRINTING Letterpress - 8x12 Chandler & Price Old Style
A bleed solid of black was screen printed on the back of the cards. The edges of the cards were colored in a hot pink to match the pink on the front of the card.
DESIGNER *Jacob Pierce*

NEW ORLEANS WEDDING INVITATION SET · 2009 · INVITATION *(right page, bottom)*
CLIENT Monica & Gregory PRINTER Dolce Press PRINTING Letterpress - Heidelberg Windmill 10x15
Invitations combine letterpress pieces into a custom enclosure with double-mounted invitation and custom-lined envelope.

A. Micah Smith ⟿

WEDDING INVITATION · 2008 · INVITATION *(right page, top)*
CLIENT Private PRINTER Vahalla Studios PRINTING Screen-printing press
Two-color print on 100# natural stock. Five pieces including a die-cut folder and belly-band holder.

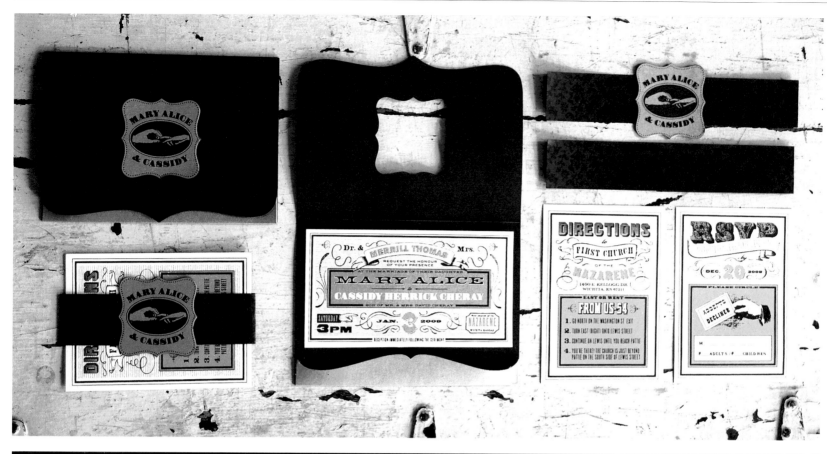

Stitch Design Co. ↶

LIBRARY: ARCHIVES OF FASHION · 2009 · STATIONARY *(top)*
CLIENT Lauren Lail PRINTER Crayton Printing PRINTING Letterpress
DESIGNER *Amy Pastre, Courtney Rowson*

SIDESHOW PRESS STATIONARY · 2009 · STATIONARY *(left)*
CLIENT Sideshow Press PRINTER Sideshow Press PRINTING Letterpress / Sewing machine
DESIGNER *Amy Pastre, Courtney Rowson*

SANDY LANG COLLATERAL · 2006 · STATIONARY *(bottom left)*
CLIENT Sandy Lang PRINTER Sideshow Press PRINTING Letterpress / Stickers
DESIGNER *Amy Pastre, Courtney Rowson*

O'HANLAN WEDDING · 2008 · INVITATION *(bottom right)*
CLIENT Sarah O'Hanlan PRINTER Sideshow Press PRINTING Letterpress / Silkscreen
DESIGNER *Amy Pastre, Courtney Rowson*

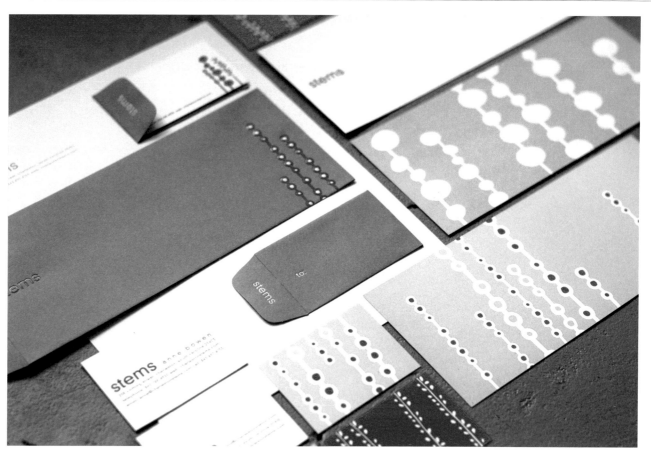

Stitch Design Co. ↝

STEMS COLLATERAL · 2009 · STATIONARY *(top)*
CLIENT Anne Bowen PRINTER Crayton Printing PRINTING Letterpress / Offset / Foil stamp
DESIGNER *Amy Pastre, Courtney Rowson*

PAKIS REHEARSAL DINNER · 2008 · INVITATION *(left)*
CLIENT Courtney Pakis PRINTER Sideshow Press PRINTING Letterpress / Cork
DESIGNER *Amy Pastre, Courtney Rowson*

PAKIS WEDDING · 2008 · INVITATION *(bottom)*
CLIENT Courtney Pakis PRINTER Sideshow Press PRINTING Letterpress / Wood / Leather cord
DESIGNER *Amy Pastre, Courtney Rowson*

The Society of Revisionist Typographers ✢

ASSORTED PRINTS · 2009 · ART PRINTS *(top)*
CLIENT Personal PRINTER SORT PRINTING Silkscreen / Letterpress
PHOTOGRAPH *Jamie Trounce*

TYPESET HUZZAH CARD · 2008 · GREETING CARD *(left)*
CLIENT Personal PRINTER SORT PRINTING Letterpress

TYPESET MOUSTACHE CARD · 2008 · GREETING CARD *(bottom)*
CLIENT Personal PRINTER SORT PRINTING Letterpress

The Society of Revisionist Typographers ~

SORT SCRIBBLE NOTEBOOK · 2009 · NOTEBOOKS *(top right, 2 images)*
CLIENT Personal   PRINTER SORT   PRINTING Letterpress

SORT STATIONERY SETS · 2009 · STATIONERY *(top left)*
CLIENT Personal   PRINTER SORT   PRINTING Letterpress

SORT IDEA PADS PACK · 2008 · 4 NOTEBOOKS *(bottom)*
CLIENT Personal   PRINTER SORT   PRINTING Letterpress

SORT NAUTICAL STATIONERY SET · 2009 · STATIONERY *(bottom left)*
CLIENT Personal   PRINTER SORT   PRINTING Letterpress

Hello Tenfold ⌣

DESIGNER · 2009 · WEDDING INVITATION *(top, 2 images)*
CLIENT Erin Allingham & Jason Bissey PRINTER Hello Tenfold PRINTING Gocco
DESIGNER *Ellie Snow*

Identity Kitchen ⌣

LISA CARPENTER PHOTOGRAPHY IDENTITY · 2009 · BUSINESS CARD *(upper left)*
CLIENT Lisa Carpenter Photography PRINTER Anemone Letterpress PRINTING Letterpress
DESIGNER *Ellen Petty*

DOUG MIRANDA PHOTOGRAPHY IDENTITY · 2008 · BUSINESS CARD *(lower left)*
CLIENT Doug Miranda Photography PRINTER Anemone Letterpress PRINTING Letterpress
DESIGNER *Ellen Petty*

JUSTINE UNGARO PHOTOGRAPHY IDENTITY · 2009 · BUSINESS CARD *(bottom)*
CLIENT Justine Ungaro PRINTER Anemone Letterpress PRINTING Letterpress
DESIGNER *Ellen Petty*

Funnel: Eric Kass ◞

FIGURE 53 SOFTWARE STATIONERY · 2009 · STATIONERY (top)
CLIENT Figure 53 PRINTER Rohner Letterpress / Faulkenberg Printing PRINTING Letterpress
Figure 53 makes QLab, award-winning software that makes it simple to create rich multimedia designs for live performances and installations. From Broadway to Britain's West End, from Denver to Denmark, QLab is the tool of choice for many of the world's most prominent designers. Letterpress silver printed + spot color offset stationery.

MARLYNE ALEXANDER PHOTOGRAPHY · 2009 · BUSINESS CARD (left)
CLIENT Marlyne Alexander Photography PRINTER Faulkenberg Printing PRINTING Letterpress

WEDDING TELEVISION CINEMATOGRAPHY · 2009 · BUSINESS CARD (bottom)
CLIENT Wedding Television PRINTER Faulkenberg Printing / D.E. Baugh PRINTING Letterpress

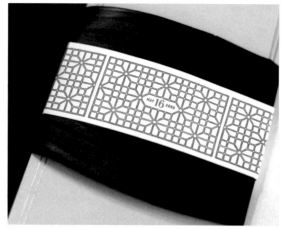

Stitch Design Co. ↝

LIVPOV BATMITZVAH · 2009 · INVITATION *(top left)*
CLIENT Lipov PRINTER Sideshow Press PRINTING Silkscreen
DESIGNER *Amy Pastre, Courtney Rowson*

LOWCOUNTRY FIELD FEAST · 2009 · INVITE *(top right)*
CLIENT Lowcountry Local First PRINTER Sideshow Press PRINTING Letterpress / Tomato seeds
DESIGNER *Amy Pastre, Courtney Rowson*

COURTNEY TEA · 2008 · INVITATION *(left)*
CLIENT Courtney Rowson PRINTER Sideshow Press PRINTING Letterpress / Tea bags attached
DESIGNER *Amy Pastre*

WORSHAM SAVE THE DATE · 2008 · SAVE THE DATE *(bottom)*
CLIENT Worsham PRINTER Sideshow Press PRINTING Letterpress / Banana leaves / Foil stamp
DESIGNER *Amy Pastre, Courtney Rowson*

Stitch Design Co. ↜

THE LEE BROS. · 2009 · PARTY MATERIAL *(top left)*
CLIENT The Lee Bros. PRINTER Sideshow Press PRINTING Letterpress / Wood
DESIGNER *Amy Pastre, Courtney Rowson*

OTTO BIRTH ANNOUNCEMENT · 2008 · BIRTH ANNOUNCEMENT *(top right)*
CLIENT Otto Pastre PRINTER Sideshow Press PRINTING Letterpress / Flipbook
DESIGNER *Amy Pastre*

LIBRARY WEDDING · 2009 · INVITATION *(middle right)*
CLIENT Elizabeth Krans PRINTER Sideshow Press PRINTING Letterpress
DESIGNER *Amy Pastre*

DAY OF THE DEAD · 2007 · INVITATION *(bottom)*
CLIENT Robert & Rachel Prioleau PRINTER Sideshow Press PRINTING Letterpress / Sewing machine
DESIGNER *Amy Pastre, Courtney Rowson*

Funnel: Eric Kass ⋄

FUNNEL CALLING CARD · 2009 · CARD *(top)*
CLIENT Funnel : Eric Kass PRINTER Rohner Letterpress PRINTING Letterpress
Random hand-punched holes on each piece.

AWKWARD BEAUTY CALLING CARD · 2009 · CARD *(bottom right)*
CLIENT Awkward Beauty: T'ai Rising-Moore PRINTER Rohner Letterpress / Faulkenberg Printing
PRINTING Letterpress

Dolce ⋄

KINETIC LENS BUSINESS CARD · 2009 · BUSINESS CARD *(right)*
CLIENT Kinetic Lens Photography PRINTER Dolce Press PRINTING Letterpress - 8x12 Chandler
& Price Old Style
Letterpress-printed on thick cotton stock with a combination of two red inks and a blind deboss.

Nate Yates ⋄

AIGA SAN DIEGO Y-CONFERENCE · 2008 · INVITATION *(bottom left)*
CLIENT AIGA San Diego PRINTER In To Ink PRINTING Letterpress
STUDIO *Conover* ART DIRECTOR *David Conover* DESIGNER *Nate Yates*

Lunalux ✴

ORNATE THANK-YOU NOTE · 2009 · GREETING CARD *(top)*
CLIENT Lunalux PRINTER Lunalux PRINTING Letterpress - Heidelberg windmill
Letterpress-printed match gray and blue on Strathmore 88# bright white wove finish bristol cover.
DESIGNER *Jenni Undis*

Product Superior ✴

PRODUCT SUPERIOR BUSINESS CARD · 2009 · DIE-CUT BUSINESS CARD *(left)*
CLIENT Product Superior Ltd. PRINTER Cranky Pressman PRINTING Letterpress
We set out to create a business card that was not only memorable, but well-designed. By having a custom die made and letterpress printing the card, we strove to make it feel more like a more tangible artifact, versus a standard smooth rectangle. Business card is custom die-cut and letterpress printed with vegetable-based ink on recycled stock.
DESIGNER *Jennifer Blanco / Product Superior Ltd.*

Funnel: Eric Kass ✴

SAARINEN CALLING CARD · 2007 · CALLING CARD *(bottom left)*
CLIENT Saarinen Artist Reps PRINTER Capitol Press PRINTING Letterpress

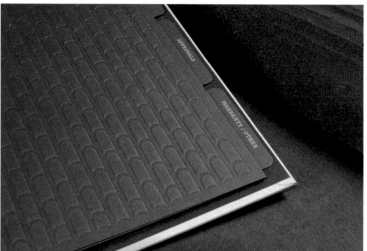

Nate Yates ✌

THOMPSON THIN BRICK · 2008 · BROCHURE *(top left)*
CLIENT Thompson Building Materials PRINTER SOS Printing PRINTING Letterpress
STUDIO *Conover* ART DIRECTOR *David Conover* DESIGNER *Nate Yates*

REDLAND CLAY TILE BINDER · 2008 · BINDER *(top right)*
CLIENT Redland Clay Tile PRINTING Letterpress
STUDIO *Conover* ART DIRECTOR *David Conover* DESIGNER *Nate Yates*

VALERY'S ROUND TUIT · 2007 · PACKAGING *(middle)*
CLIENT Conover PRINTER In To Ink PRINTING Letterpress
STUDIO *Conover* ART DIRECTOR *David Conover* DESIGNER *Nate Yates*

Funnel: Eric Kass ✌

SOMERSAULTS CALLING CARD · 2008 · CARD *(bottom)*
CLIENT Somersaults Life Archives PRINTER Stumptown Printers / Faulkenberg Printing

Dolce ℘

FEATHERED FLOURISH STATIONERY · 2008 · STATIONERY (*middle left*)
CLIENT Helene & Jerry PRINTER Dolce Press PRINTING Letterpress - Heidelberg Windmill 10x15
Custom letterpress stationery printed on cotton papercreased to permit folding. Matching envelopes also printed and lined with matching liners.

VIVIAN DOAN · 2008 · CD COVER (*middle right*)
CLIENT Vivian Doan Photography PRINTER Dolce Press PRINTING Letterpress - Heidelberg Windmill 10x15
Custom covers for CDs that the client hands out to her customers with her photos on it.
DESIGNER Vivian Doan

Tota Press ℘

AUGUST 2009 · 2009 · ALL-OCCASION GREETING CARD (*top*)
CLIENT Personal PRINTER Tota Press PRINTING Letterpress - Vandercook
Inspired by my family and by nature.

SEPTEMBER 2009 · 2009 · ALL-OCCASION GREETING CARD (*bottom*)
CLIENT Personal PRINTER Tota Press PRINTING Letterpress - Vandercook
An ode to the spirit of water.

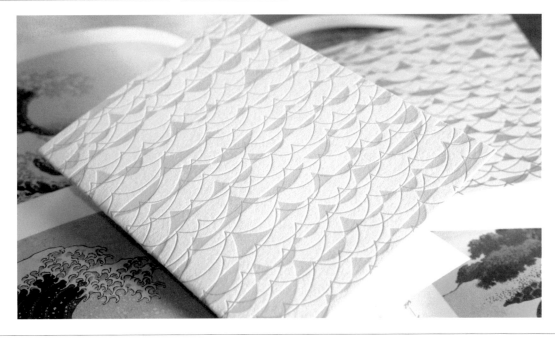

Public Domain ꙳

BRAD & AMANDA'S WEDDING · 2008 · INVITATION *(top)*
CLIENT Brad & Amanda   PRINTING Screen-print
Two-color Screen-print wedding invitation on craft paper stock.
DESIGNER *Matt Pamer*

DEAR DEAR EP · 2008 · PACKAGING *(bottom)*
CLIENT Dear Dear   PRINTING Screen-print
Two-color sreen-printed EP packaging with hand-applied sticker.
DESIGNER *Matt Pamer*

Type B Press ꙳

EMILY DUNBAR CD ALBUM · 2009 · PACKAGING *(right & bottom left)*
CLIENT Emily Dunbar   PRINTER Type B Press   PRINTING Letterpress - 12x18 Chandler & Price
The packaging was hand-printed from metal letterpress cuts/plates on Stumptown Printers blank chipboard packaging. The tactile nature of letterpress and the natural feel of the chipboard fit well with Emily's folk-music style.

Sightlab ∿

SELF-PROMOTION · 2009 · BUSINESS CARD *(top)*
CLIENT Personal PRINTING Embossing / Die-cut

Public Domain ∿

A COSMONAUT'S RUIN EP SLEEVE · 2009 · PACKAGING *(right, 2 images)*
CLIENT A Cosmonaut's Ruin PRINTING Screen-print
Screen-print 7" record sleeve. The ink is glow in the dark.
DESIGNER *Matt Pamer*

LOCKS OF LOVE POSTER · 2007 · POSTER *(bottom left)*
CLIENT Locks of Love PRINTING Screen-print
One-color Screen-print poster on orange stock.
DESIGNER *Matt Pamer*

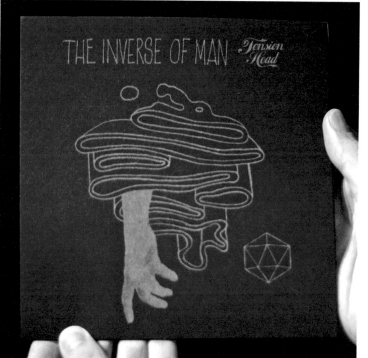

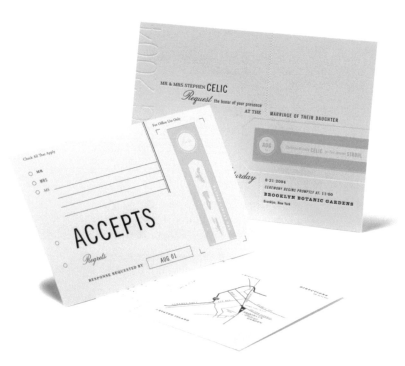

Silnt ᠊

HONG KONG HANDSHAKE · 2007 · BUSINESS CARD *(top)*
CLIENT SILNT PRINTER Kai Lian Printing PRINTING Letterpress
White & gold foil stamping on white Shirio 80, 1400 gsm. Duplexing of white Shirio 80, 700 gsm.
DESIGNER *Felix Ng*

DISTILLERY BUSINESS CARDS · 2008 · BUSINESS CARD *(lower left)*
CLIENT Distillery Studio PRINTER Kai Lian Printing PRINTING Letterpress
The business card is designed by silkscreening a custom-mixed metallic bronze ink and PMS 491 U on 220 gsm New Raglin paper. Distillery's existing logo is applied as an accent using blind-emboss, allowing the details of the logo to be seen subtly on both sides.
DESIGNER *Felix Ng*

ART WITH SOUND BOX SET · 2009 · ALBUM COVER *(middle right)*
CLIENT Dual City Sessions PRINTER Kai Lian Printing PRINTING Letterpress
We designed a special-edition box set containing the 10 artworks and 10 sounds created by the participating artists for our curated exhibition, Dual City Sessions / Art with Sound.
Packaging: 1290 gsm cardboard (Germany), artworks printed on: 300 gsm recycled FSC-certified Wove Fresh White, set in Alt Haas Grotesk, edition: 100 cps
DESIGNER *Felix Ng*

Christine Celic Strohl & Eric Strohl ᠊

CELIC / STROHL WEDDING • 2004 • INVITATION *(upper left)*
CLIENT Personal PRINTER Peter Kruty Editions PRINTING Letterpress - Vandercook Proof Press
This wedding invitation involved several pieces, both letterpress and offset. A series of adhesive stickers were applied to the reply card and the blind emboss invitation to provide a combination of textures and to bring in the primary ceremony color.

CENTRAL CARDS • 2009 • BUSINESS CARDS *(bottom)*
CLIENT Central PRINTER One Heart Press PRINTING Letterpress
Corporate identity and stationery for a Bay Area strategy and consulting firm which focuses on craft. Printed on a thick Crane's stock, the use of blind deboss and sparse color echoes the firm's sensibilities.

dry ic...

museu...

chicago...

24 janu...

mcachi...

invitation

dry ice

6:30

RUFUS WAINWRIGHT compositeur-interprète qui travaille
actuellement à la composition de *Prima Donna*, un opéra
retraçant une journée dans la vie d'une diva à la gloire fanée...

HOLZER
ELIASSON
KOONS

Thirst ↝

DRY ICE · MCA'S ANNUAL GALA · 2008 · INVITATION *(top, right, bottom left)*
CLIENT The Museum of Contemporary Art / Chicago PRINTER Artistry Engraving, The Graphic
Arts Studio, Crosshair, Laser Excel PRINTING Offset, engraving, silkscreening, laser die-cutting
DESIGNER *Rick Valicenti*

UTOPIA · 2008 · CATALOG *(bottom right)*
CLIENT Wright Auctions PRINTER The Graphic Arts Studio PRINTING Offset
TYPE CREDITS Omnes, Joshua Darden Bau, Christian Schwartz Univers, Adrian Frutiger
DESIGN DIRECTOR *Rick Valicenti/Thirst* DESIGN *Rick Valicenti & Jennifer Mahanay/Wright*
PHOTOGRAPHY *Thea Dickman* PROGRAMMING *Robb Irrgang* RESEARCH *Emilie Sims*

Pomegranate ∽

LOVE, PEACE AND JOY · 2008 · CHRISTMAS CARD *(top left)*
HO HO HO · 2007 · CHRISTMAS CARD *(middle left)*
OUR GREEN PLEDGE · 2008 · COASTER *(middle right)*
A LITTLE WORD OF THANKS · 2008 · COASTER *(bottom left)*
BABY SHOWER – PRAM · 2009 · SINGLE PANEL INVITATION *(bottom right)*

CLIENT Personal PRINTER Pomegranate Letterpress PRINTING Letterpress · Chandler & Price Pilot · Caligo Safe-Wash Inks

DESIGNER (ALL) *Joe Borges R.G.D.*

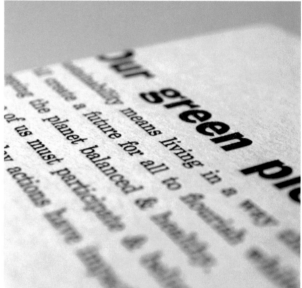

Pomegranate ✳

BACI BOX · 2009 · ADULT GAME *(top left)*
CLIENT Personal PRINTER Pomegranate Letterpress PRINTING Letterpress · Chandler & Price Pilot
A kissing game developed by Margot Cudmore. Letterpressed box and game pieces, all die-cut into hearts.

POME CALENDAR · 2008 · CALENDAR *(top right)*
CLIENT Personal PRINTER Pomegranate Letterpress PRINTING Letterpress · Chandler & Price Pilot
Vintage metal moveable type calendar. Typeset with metal/wood type and icons. Caligo Safe-Wash Inks.

FERNANDO PESSOA · 2007 · GREETING CARD *(middle left)*
CLIENT Personal PRINTER Pomegranate Letterpress PRINTING Letterpress · Chandler & Price Pilot
Letters from a Pessoa poem were designed into a portrait. Caligo Safe-Wash Inks.

TULIPS · 2008 · GREETING CARD *(middle right)*
CLIENT Personal PRINTER Pomegranate Letterpress PRINTING Letterpress · Chandler & Price Pilot
Illustration based on dingbat from the Lisboa font. Caligo Safe-Wash Inks.

MOST WONDERFUL TIME · 2008 · CHRISTMAS CARD *(bottom right)*
CLIENT Personal PRINTER Pomegranate Letterpress PRINTING Letterpress · Chandler & Price Pilot

DESIGNER (ALL) *Joe Borges R.G.D.*

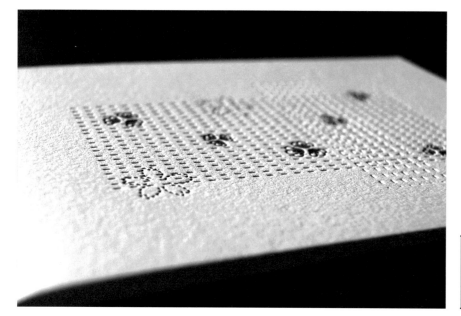

Satsuma ·

STATIONARY · 2009 · CARDS
CLIENT Personal PRINTING Letterpress

PEACE

Satsuma ↝

STATIONARY · 2009 · CARDS
CLIENT Personal PRINTING Letterpress

Kamal ✄

MODERN DOTS · 2009 · GREETING CARD *(top)*
STARBURST · 2009 · GREETING CARD *(left)*
TURQUOISE AND YELLOW PEACOCK · 2009 · GREETING CARD *(bottom)*
CLIENT Personal PRINTING Letterpress
All graphics are original pieces of work, hand drawn, scanned, then traced on the computer.

Kamal ᴧ

SKY TEXTILE · 2009 · GREETING CARD *(top left)*
SKY PINWHEEL · 2009 · GREETING CARD *(top right)*
COASTER BACKS · 2009 · COASTERS *(bottom)*
CLIENT Personal PRINTING Letterpress
All graphics are original pieces of work, hand drawn, scanned, then traced on the computer.

Soulseven ↝

FAME BRANDING BAR PARTY · 2009 · **INVITATION & ENVELOPE** *(top)*
CLIENT Fame PRINTER Studio On Fire PRINTING Letterpress
The "dive bar" theme was integrated throughout the campaign, including: letterpress invitation, bar kit consisting of gold-leaf matchbooks and coasters, promo posters, e-mail blast, and the office environment.
DESIGNER/ILLUSTRATOR *Sam Soulek* CREATIVE DIRECTOR *Bruce Edwards* COPYWRITER *Chris Yocum*
AGENCY *FAME - A Retail Branding Agency*

TARGET - WORLD'S TOUGHEST COWBOY · 2007 · **BANDANA & FLYER** *(left)*
CLIENT Target Corporation PRINTING Screen-print
Promotional materials for a traveling rodeo and reality TV show, called "World's Toughest Cowboy". We also created a print ad campaign and a viral ad for promoting the TV show premiere.
DESIGNER/ILLUSTRATOR *Sam Soulek* CREATIVE DIRECTOR *Bruce Edwards* COPYWRITER *Julie Feyerer*
AGENCY *FAME - A Retail Branding Agency*

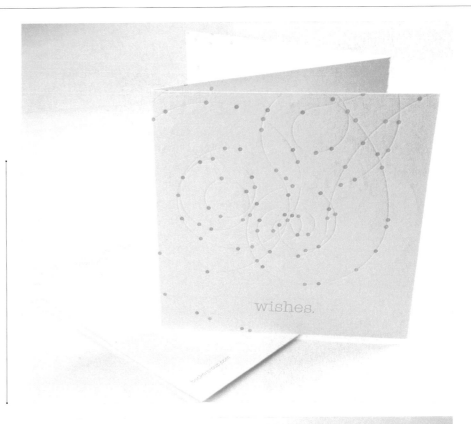

Soulseven ↝

BECKER GROUP · 2008 · HOLIDAY CARD *(top)*
CLIENT Becker Group PRINTER Studio On Fire PRINTING Letterpress
Becker Group is an experiential marketing company that takes brands and turns them into environments for consumers.
DESIGNER/ILLUSTRATOR *Sam Soulek* CREATIVE DIRECTOR *Bruce Edwards* COPYWRITER *Julie Feyerer*
AGENCY *FAME - A Retail Branding Agency*

FAME - ECO FREAKO CAMPAIGN · 2008 · GUIDEBOOK *(bottom)*
CLIENT Fame PRINTING Screen-print
FAME - A Retail Branding Agency was charged by their holdings company to lower their carbon footprint, and needed a brand created to get it's employees excited about going green. It was important to minimize the environmental impact when producing the brand materials, so great care was taken to calculate the cost of printing, producing and shipping. Printing was done using pieces of left-over office scrap for the invitation/tags, posters and pins. Reusable bags for lunches, water glasses and coffee mugs helped us lower our trash output. A signing system was also created for recycling receptacles throughout the agency.
DESIGNER/ILLUSTRATOR *Jessica Keintz, Sam Soulek* CREATIVE DIRECTOR *Cheryl Meyer* COPYWRITER *Julie Feyerer* AGENCY *FAME - A Retail Branding Agency*

Brian Danaher ◆

CLUTTER BEAR RECORDS CORPORATE ID · 2008 · STATIONERY *(top)*
CLIENT Clutter Bear Records PRINTER Spark Print Solutions PRINTING Letterpress

Sycamore Street Press ◆

2010 CALENDAR · 2009 · POSTER *(bottom, 2 images)*
CLIENT Personal PRINTER Sycamore Street Press PRINTING Letterpress - Vandercook #3
We printed this using soy inks and cotton paper made from reclaimed fibers.
DESIGNER *Eva Jorgensen for {Folk} by Sycamore Street Press*

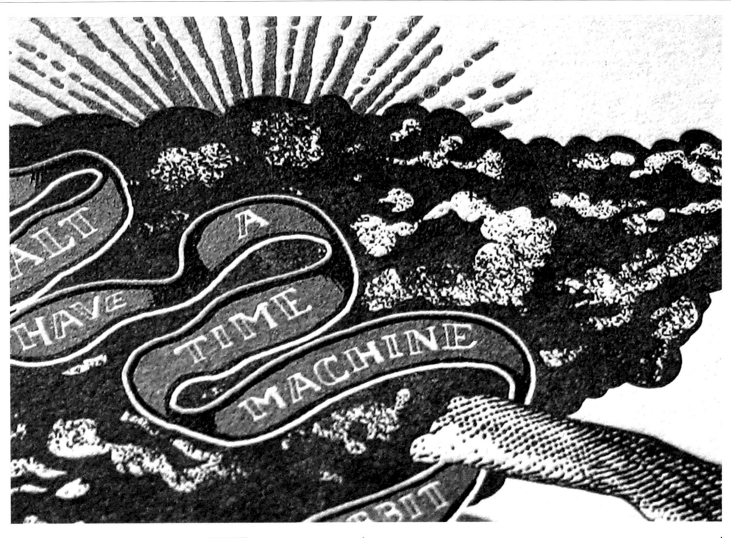

Brian Danaher ⌁

RABBIT CHILDREN · 2009 · CD PACKAGE
CLIENT Clutter Bear Records PRINTER Spark Print Solutions PRINTING Letterpress
CD package cover detail

Enormous Champion ⌁

SKELETON KEYS · 2009 · ART PRINT *(top, bottom)*
ONE TO GROW ON · 2008 · FOUR-BAR GREETING CARD *(right)*
CLIENT Personal PRINTER Enormous Champion PRINTING Letterpress · Vandercook Universal I

Enormous Champion ✒

A MIS-TAPE · 2008 · FOUR-BAR GREETING CARD *(top)*
CLIENT Personal PRINTER Enormous Champion PRINTING Letterpress · Vandercook Universal I

Bandito Design Co. ✒

FANCY SKULL · 2009 · POSTER *(right)*
LOVE WHAT YOU DO... · 2009 · POSTER *(bottom)*
CLIENT Personal PRINTER Bandito Design Co. PRINTING Letterpress

Bespoke Press ↝

HER LOVE'S A PONY · 2009 · ART PRINT *(top left)*
CLIENT The Bespoke Illustrators Project PRINTER Bespoke Letterpress Boutique PRINTING Letterpress - 1893 Chandler & Price Oldstyle Platen
Printed on 100% Cotton rag stocks.
DESIGNER *Kristal Melson*

UNTITLED · 2009 · ART PRINT *(top right)*
CLIENT The Bespoke Illustrators Project PRINTER Bespoke Letterpress Boutique PRINTING Letterpress - 1893 Chandler & Price Oldstyle Platen
Printed on 100% Cotton rag stocks.

Ben Whitla ↝

THE BLOW · 2005 · FLYER *(bottom left)*
CLIENT The Eaves PRINTER Boxcar Press PRINTING Letterpress - Heidelberg Windmill

BONFIRE MADIGAN · 2005 · FLYER *(bottom left)*
CLIENT The Eaves PRINTER Boxcar Press PRINTING Letterpress - Heidelberg Windmill
Paper is duplex white over crimson with gold letterpress Eaves logo on back.

Swink ✎

CAMPFIRE ON YOUR DESKTOP - SELF-PROMOTION • 2009 • KIT
CLIENT Swink PRINTER Studio on Fire PRINTING Letterpress
DESIGNER *Shanan Galligan, Drew Garza, Yogie Jacala*

Hello! 608.442.8899
swinkinc.com
WE ARE SWINK.

SWINK

Nothing's better than a campfire and a good story.
- - - - - - - - - - - - - - - -
Bring your beer, your buns, a little
inspiration, and come join us. We're
imaginative folks and we love stories.
re at Swink, we know the
dy exists

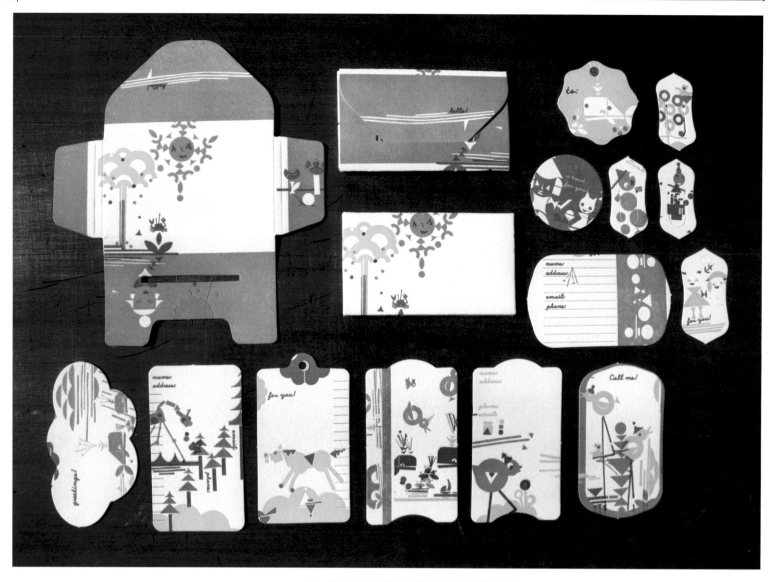

Studio on Fire ⌒

UNTITLED · 2008 · STATIONARY SET
CLIENT Personal PRINTER Studio On Fire PRINTING Letterpress
DESIGNER *Kelly English, Kindra Murphy*

HOMAGE   TO   THE   STAMP

DEUTSCHE
BUNDESPOST

DEUTSCHE BUNDESPOST

DEUTSCHE BUNDESPOST

60

60   60

DEUTSCHE
BUNDESPOST

DEUTSCHE
BUNDESPOST

DEUTSCHE
BUNDESPOST

60

60

DEUTSCHE
BUNDESPOST

DEUTSCHE
BUNDESPOST

BY

GAVIN

POTENZA

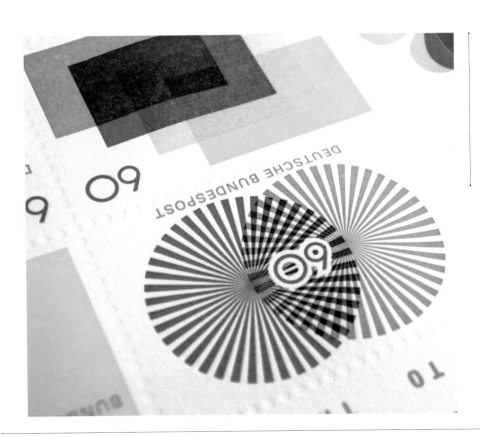

Gavin Potenza ⌁

HOMAGE TO THE STAMP · 2008 · ART PRINT *(this page, 2 images)*
CLIENT Tiny Showcase PRINTER DWRI Letterpress PRINTING Letterpress
The artwork has been printed on an archival 250 gsm Somerset Radiant White printmaking paper.
It contains four overlapping transparent print layers and one blind debossed layer. Limited to an
edition of 200, each print is blind debossed with the edition number.

NORGE LETTERPRESS · 2009 · ART PRINT *(right page)*
CLIENT Personal PRINTER Fortress Letterpress PRINTING Letterpress
A 5x7" letterpress print. Edition of 60, 2 colors on 110 lb eggshell cotton paper with a special blind
debossed edge providing a subtle raised effect for the stamp itself.

NORGE 3⁰⁰

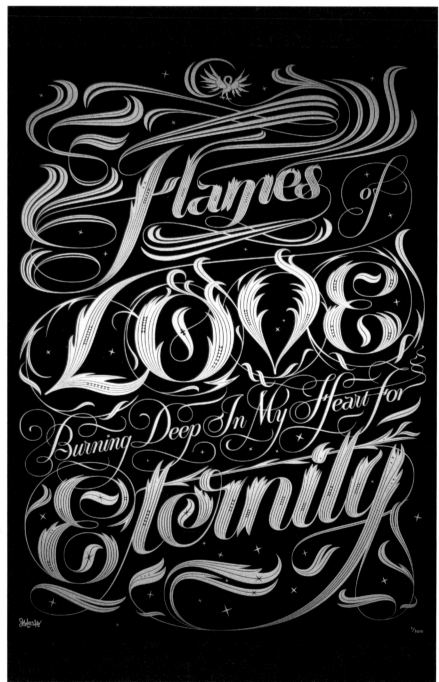

Seb Lester

HELLFIRE · 2009 · LIMITED EDITION PRINT (top left)
CLIENT Personal PRINTING Screen-print
The Hellfire Club was the popular name for a number of clubs for high-society rakes established all over Britain and Ireland in the 18th century. A2 edition of 100 on Satin Mirri, 160 gsm paper.

ARSE · 2009 · LIMITED EDITION PRINT (top right)
CLIENT Personal PRINTING Screen-print
Set in an exquisite 19th century "Alphabet of Love". Apparently Shakespeare used the word "arse" in Romeo & Juliet. A1 edition of 100. Black & gold on Bright White Colorplan Smooth paper, 270 gsm. Blind embossed for authenticity.

FLAMES · 2009 · LIMITD EDITION PRINT (left)
CLIENT Personal PRINTING Screen-print
"Flames" is about big concepts. Love, life and eternity. A1 edition of 100. Metallic gold ink on black Plike, 240 gsm.

HOME SWEET HOME · 2009 · ART PRINT (bottom)
CLIENT Personal PRINTING Screen-print
Limited-edition version is printed on a very expensive paper that changes colour depending on the angle it is viewed at. Square unsigned open edition. Carbon black ink on Bright White Colorplan Smooth paper, 270 gsm.

BELIEVE · 2008 · LIMITED EDITION PRINT (right page)
CLIENT Personal PRINTING Screen-print
It is all about passion, focus, and commitment. A2 edition of 100. Blue, metallic silver, and black on Colorplan Smooth paper, 270 gsm.

Ohio Pride

DON'T LOSE HEART

The 4 chambers of love that drive the U.S. of A.

216 & 330

Use this coaster to enjoy a pop or a delicious Great Lakes™ Beer.

No. 17

PLACE POP HERE

Mike Burton

DON'T LOSE HEART · 2007 · COASTER *(top & left)*
CLIENT Mikey Burton & Cranky Pressman PRINTER Cranky Pressman PRINTING Letterpress - Original Heidelberg
A letterpress coaster to cross promote Mikey Burton and the Cranky Pressman. Go Ohio!

CRANKY PRESSMAN SKULL PRESS · 2009 · LOGO *(right)*
CLIENT Cranky Pressman PRINTER Cranky Pressman PRINTING Letterpress - Original Heidelberg
Icon for launch of Cranky Pressman 2.0.

CRANKY PRESSMAN PROMO · 2007 · POSTCARD *(right page)*
CLIENT Cranky Pressman PRINTER Cranky Pressman PRINTING Letterpress - Original Heidelberg
For years, an old letterpress craftsman fought for survival in a place called The Rustbelt. Then one day a passing soul spoke of a promised land called the internet. The craftsman saw hope through his very nearsighted lenses, and CrankyPressman.com was conceived.
ART DIRECTOR *Jamie Berger.*

FORTRESS

PREMIUM QUALITY HAND CRAFTED

ART CRANK

EST.   2008

TRADE   MARK

09

MADE IN PORTLAND OR

FORTRESSLETTERPRESS.BLOGSPOT.COM

The Paper Nut ✧

ABCs, BIRDS, GIRAFFES, SUNS · 2008 · GREETING CARDS *(this page)*
CLIENT Personal PRINT Tryst Press PRINTING Letterpress - Vandercook SP 15
DESIGNER *Jeanie Nelson*

Fortress Letterpress

BUZZ WORDS · 2009 · POSTER *(left page)*
CLIENT Art Crank PRINTER Fortress Letterpress PRINTING Letterpress - 8x12 Chandler & Price
DESIGNER *Bruce Paulson*

alberto
Cerriteño

Cerriteño 09

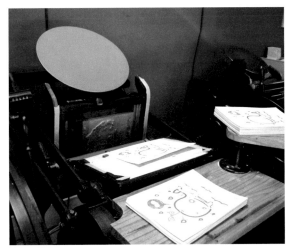

Alberto Cerriteño ❧

THE ENAMORED WHALE · 2009 · POSTER
CLIENT Personal PRINTER Studio Olivine PRINTING Letterpress - Chandler & Price

Studio On Fire ⤴

CARDLINE · 2007 · CARDS *(3 images)*
CLIENT Personal PRINTER Studio On Fire PRINTING Letterpress
DESIGNER *Rinzen*

Studio On Fire ↺

TEN YEAR ANNIVERSARY • 2009 • POSTER *(left, 2 images)*
CLIENT Personal PRINTER Studio On Fire PRINTING Letterpress
DESIGNER *Benjamin Levitz*

CARDLINE · 2007 · CARDS *(right, 2 images)*
CLIENT Personal PRINTER Studio On Fire PRINTING Letterpress
DESIGNER *Rinzen*

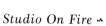

Studio On Fire ⌃

CARDLINE · 2007 · CARDS
CLIENT Personal PRINTER Studio On Fire PRINTING Letterpress
DESIGNER *Adam Garcia (The Pressure)*

Studio On Fire ❧

CARDLINE · 2007 · CARDS
CLIENT Personal PRINTER Studio On Fire PRINTING Letterpress
DESIGNER *Brian Gunderson (top, bottom left)*
DESIGNER *Aesthetic Apparatus (bottom right)*

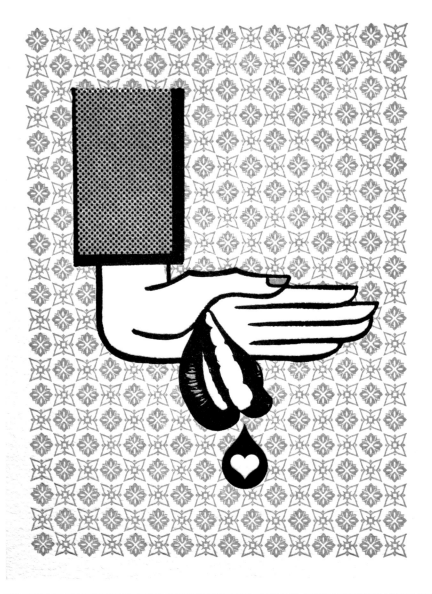

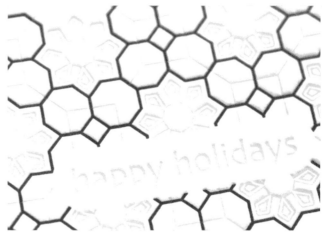

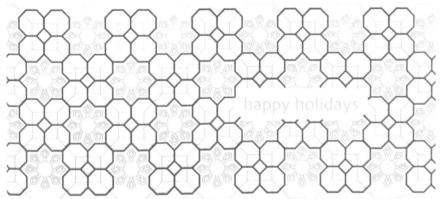

Tiselle ~

MOSAIC SNOWFLAKE · 2008 · GREETING CARD *(top, 2 images)*
BEIJING OPERA SINGER · 2007 · GREETING CARD *(bottom left)*
BAROQUE JOY · 2008 · GREETING CARD *(bottom right)*
CLIENT Personal PRINTER Tiselle Letterpress PRINTING Letterpress - Vandercook SP 15
DESIGNER *Tianyi Wang* PHOTO *Steven Lam Photography*

Tiselle ~

FISH · 2007 · GREETING CARD *(top left)*
CICADA · 2007 · GREETING CARD *(top left)*
REGRETFUL OWL · 2008 · GREETING CARD *(bottom left)*
PARTRIDGE IN A PEAR TREE · 2008 · GREETING CARD *(bottom right)*
CLIENT Personal PRINTER Tiselle Letterpress PRINTING Letterpress - Vandercook SP 15
DESIGNER *Tianyi Wang* PHOTO: *Steven Lam Photography*

Merry christmas

I'm sorry

Studio On Fire •ⁱ•

THE BRAINCHILD OF BEN LEVITZ, MINNEAPOLIS-BASED PRINT SHOP STUDIO ON FIRE SCENTS OUT THE ELUSIVE GHOST IN THE MACHINE – AND BREATHES NEW LIFE INTO OLD PRESSES, PAPER STOCK, AND TECHNIQUES. WITH A KEEN EYE FOR BOTH PRODUCTION PITFALLS AND DESIGN RULES, THE STUDIO'S PRINTER-DESIGNERS COMBINE A PLETHORA OF TECHNIQUES— DIE CUTTING, MATRIX SCORING, STOCK DUPLEXING AND EDGE COLOURING—TO ADD ANOTHER DIMENSION OR LAYER OF PERCEPTION WHERE WE LEAST EXPECT IT. IN THIS, THEY MOVE BEYOND THE ARCHETYPAL LETTERPRESS AESTHETICS AND COLOR SCHEMES: THEIR SPOT-ON CONTEMPORARY ILLUSTRATIONS ARE NOT AVERSE TO THE ODD SPLASHES OF ACID COLOR, INTRICATE TRACING OR IRREVERENT SUBJECTS.

···> *What is your background in design and printmaking?*

I have come to letterpress printing from two directions: as a kid that loved machines and as a graphic designer. I grew up welding, building go-carts, and fixing things on a small Minnesota farm. Later on, I studied Fine Arts in Communication Design. After just one year as a graphic designer, I found myself longing to get away from the chained-to-the-computer lifestyle to build something with a good old-fashioned arc welder instead. When I visited a friend's studio who had this old hand-fed printing press sitting right next to his computer, it was like an epiphany—machines and design living together! So, to my wife's surprise, I went out and bought a printing press to start a print shop in the basement of our home, between the boiler and the cat litter box. By 2006, it had grown to several tons of machines that occupied a full studio space in an arts building. It was evident that my letterpress hobby was eclipsing my design career so I devoted my full attention to building a hybrid print and design studio. The studio now employs several people very committed to merging design and production with a focus on the unique characteristics of letterpress. Approaching this particular printing process as designers gives us a special understanding of what designers expect from their finished product. In the end, that is what drives what we work on and who we work with—great design.

···> *Do you remember your first brush with letterpress?*

During my senior thesis project, I was researching a sans serif type design by W.A. Dwiggins and investigated the history of sans serif type development. Dwiggins had designed his Metro typeface for casting in hot metal. I was fascinated by the process of drawing letters, cutting punches, and ultimately casting the letters in metal for letterpress printing.

···> *Let's get technical: What kind of press(es) or machinery do you use and what are their particular attributes, advantages, or drawbacks?*

We use Heidelberg, Heidelberg, and more Heidelberg. Both cylinder and platen presses are staples at our shop. These German presses are arguably the best letter-press machines ever built. They have superior ability to register work tightly and quickly set to auto-feed the wide variety of materials we print on—from napkin tissue to heavy coaster stocks and book board. They can run many thousands of impressions a day. We also use a few Vandercook cylinder presses. These are ideal for high-quality but small-quantity projects like wedding invitations and poster editions. Not to forget our very first type of printing press, a Chandler and Price 10x15 platen jobber, which is still busy with hand-fed projects.

···> *Could you take us through the actual printing and production process?*

Production of a letterpress project takes finesse and attention to the smallest details. The steps are as follows:

ESTIMATING AND PLANNING PRODUCTION: This is actually one of the most time-intensive parts of production and a key part of the design process. Aspects like color and type of paper stock, the size of a final piece, and the right combination of production methods and letterpress printing are vital to the process.

FILMING: We take a vector-based computer artwork file, lay out the press sheet on the computer and send a proof to the client. Then, a piece of high-resolution and high-density image-setter film negative is produced for each color in a design. This film is then used as an overlay to expose the plate material.

PLATING: For the making of our printing plates we use a light-sensitive plastic called photopolymer. The film negative is placed on top of this polymer sheet, both are sealed together on a vacuum table and then exposed to UV light. After exposure, the negative is removed and the polymer sheet is placed in a water bath to remove and dissolve the unexposed areas, leaving behind the raised printing surface. The plate is carefully dried and re-exposed to UV light to make it hard enough to produce an impression. Our plates are backed with a sheet of strong adhesive that allows them to stick to the metal base in the printing press.

PRINTING: The final polymer plate is positioned in the printing press and the press is inked up. Then the printing begins, carefully monitoring color and impression. A separate pass through the press is required for each color in the design.

FINISHING: After the paper is printed, we trim everything to final size or add some special finishing work. Aspects like laser cutting, hot foiling, engraving, and offset printing are provided by outside studios.

···> *Any additional advice for aspiring letterpress fans?*

Avoid over-designing: Letterpress works best when it is simple. To keep costs down and make sure the design translates to the process, begin by working with a printer in the early design stages.

Solid areas of color are not ideal: Solid color is difficult to control and there will be some color variation throughout the run. Some pieces may have darker ink density than others. Elements like text, line-work, and patterns work best.

Solid areas can appear "salty": It may be necessary to print with less ink density in solid areas to keep fine details in your artwork crisp. We call the resulting mottled ink appearance "saltiness". This also depends on paper stock—darker colours on a toothy cotton stock will look more granular than light colors on a smooth stock.

Forget about gradients or color tints: As a general rule, letterpress does not allow for print gradients, i.e. a 50% color value will need to be printed as a separate spot colour.

Limitations of photographic reproductions: While single—color photographs (like a greyscale newspaper) are possible, the line screen is coarser—at around 75lpi to 100lpi.

···> *Unlike many other letterpress projects, your designs are decidedly modern. Which old-school idiosyncrasies do you cherish and retain and which ones do you consider trite and passé?*

There are a couple of things that seem to define letterpress in the minds of many people. Trite is the notion that letterpress printing is primarily for wedding designs, as popularized by Martha Stewart. Nor is it only about the visual sensibility of over-inked wood type and antique advertising cuts. The things we love about letterpress are those that make it unique as a printing method. For us, the allure of modern letterpress is in its tactility—the way the ink sits on the paper, the bite of the plate into the sheet, its texture and excellent typography. Letterpress enjoys popularity today because it can produce something that feels different. So, it does not have to be equated with one particular design vernacular. It should be embraced by designers for its unique characteristics. We strive to produce things that people will actually want and keep. This is what we love.

Studio On Fire ⌁

STATIONARY SET · 2008 · STATIONARY
CLIENT Personal PRINTER Studio On Fire PRINTING Letterpress
DESIGNER *Kelly English, Kindra Murphy*

Studio On Fire ◡

CALENDAR · 2007 (top)
CLIENT Personal PRINTER Studio On Fire PRINTING Letterpress
DESIGNER various

CALENDAR · 2008 (bottom, 3 images)
CLIENT Personal PRINTER Studio On Fire PRINTING Letterpress
DESIGNER various

Studio On Fire ↝

2008 AIGA MN DESIGN CAMP · 2008 · IDENTITY *(4 images)*
CLIENT AIGA Minnesota PRINTER Studio On Fire PRINTING Letterpress

Jan / 09

Feb / 09

Mar / 09

Jul / 09

Aug / 09

Sep / 09

Apr / 09

May / 09

Jun / 09

Oct / 09

Nov / 09

Dec / 09

Studio On Fire ∿

CALENDAR · 2009

CLIENT Personal   PRINTER Studio On Fire   PRINTING Letterpress

DESIGNERS *Gunderson Jacobs, Rinzen, Clarimus, Justin Blyth, Adam Garcia, Studio On Fire*

Studio On Fire ~

CARDLINE · 2007 · CARDS
CLIENT Personal PRINTER Studio On Fire PRINTING Letterpress
DESIGNER *Mike Perry* (top, 2 images)
DESIGNER *Emily Magnuson* (bottom left, 2 images)
DESIGNER *Clarimus* (bottom right)

Studio On Fire ⌐

CARDLINE · 2007 · CARDS
CLIENT Personal PRINTER Studio On Fire PRINTING Letterpress
DESIGNER *Dan Funderburgh* (top left, bottom left)
DESIGNER *Nothing Is Forever* (bottom middle)
DESIGNER *Rinzen* (bottom right)

POWER OF LOVE POSTER · 2008 · POSTER (top right)
CLIENT Poster Offensive 2008 PRINTER Studio On Fire PRINTING Letterpress
DESIGNER *Benjamin Levitz - Studio On Fire*

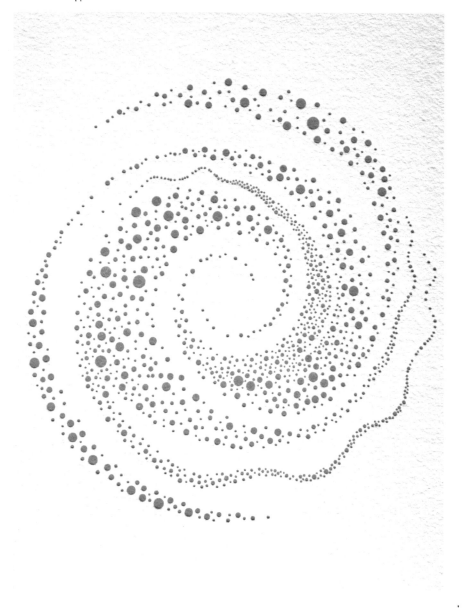

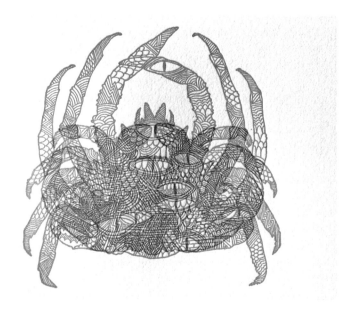

Studio On Fire ⌐

CARDLINE · 2007 · CARDS
CLIENT Personal PRINTER Studio On Fire PRINTING Letterpress
DESIGNER *Rinzen (top left)*
DESIGNER *Mike Perry (3 images)*

CARDLINE · 2007 · CARDS *(right page)*
CLIENT Personal PRINTER Studio On Fire PRINTING Letterpress
DESIGNER *Dan Funderburgh*

Cloudy Collection •⁄•

Four times a year, David Huyck invites six of his favorite illustrators to join him in a new edition of the Cloudy Collection. A work in progress—and progressive in its approach – this series of limited art prints provides a welcome beacon and silver lining within the current fog and flood of arts & crafts projects. Huyck's aim: affordable, accessible and sustainable art for all, lovingly curated by the artist himself. Imbued with this (cumulo-)nimbus of lofty ideals, his project is nevertheless firmly rooted in reality: Every edition contains seven themed, photo-frame-sized prints, the printing process is environmentally friendly, and a proportion of the proceeds goes his charity of choice, The Nature Conservancy.

···> *How did you end up in illustration and publishing? Any formative experiences?*
I have always been a doodler—I simply cannot keep my hand still if it is holding a pencil—but when I started college, I was pretty sure I was going to be a doctor or a biologist of some sort. Even so, I took a drawing class, which met in the school's print shop. Something about the smell of all those inks must have seeped into my psyche. I loved the drawing class and creating with my hands, so as soon as I could I started taking printmaking classes—we did screen-printing, lithography, etching, and relief-printing. We even had a Vandercook press and a bunch of lead type drawers. I quickly forgot about the idea of being a doctor.

My print professor, Fred, has this magical drawer filled with prints he has collected over the years from students, friends, and visiting artists, and as we were learning each new technique, we would get to see a few more tantalizing prints.

With any relief-printing technique, the plate can leave a physical indentation in the paper as it presses its ink into the page. With letterpress, that effect is even stronger because the plates or lead type are sturdy enough to take a lot of pressure. The result is that the two-dimensional image or text you have created is instantly transformed into a three-dimensional object as soon as the plate hits the paper. Even with your eyes closed, you can smell the ink and feel the image with your fingertips—it is such a sensual medium!

···> *What are you looking for in a contributor to the Cloudy Collection?*
I love finding people who are ready to play. And this applies both to my clients, who tend to have a sense of humor and are familiar with their inner child, and to the people I chose for the Collection.

Nevertheless, deciding who to invite is both the easiest and the most difficult thing in the world. While it is great to ask people I admire to collaborate, it can be very difficult to select just six new artists! Right now, I have a list of more than 100 potential contributors. The first time I invited someone I truly idolized—one of my major art crushes—I was super nervous about it. But after some wonderful and generous responses, I am not nervous about rejection anymore.

···> *And what about the chosen format?*
Besides my own work, I include six artists in each print set for a few reasons. One is that I love the process of coming up with a theme, and then picking the artists that best match the theme. It also introduces fans of one particular artist to a few others they may otherwise never encounter. Not to forget the sheer endless number of favorites—if I invited them one at a time, I would never get through that list!

At the same time, I want to produce collectable art at an affordable price. Besides the low dollar amount, all prints are the standard photo-frame size of 4" x 6", so you can just pick any inexpensive frame.

···> *Is there anything special about the printing?*
One of the main reasons I started the Cloudy Collection was because my college friend Harold Kyle owns Boxcar Press, one of the biggest letterpress shops in the U.S. He prints the Cloudy Collection on a Vandercook press. It has a big drum

that rolls the paper across the plate, which is both an efficient way of rapidly printing a big stack of paper and an effective way of gently stretching the paper along its length. One of the common troubleshooting tasks is to make sure that the second color of the print registers well with the first color because of this stretching – after the first run, the paper is not the same size anymore! In addition, you have to ensure that your details are not too fine or intricate, otherwise the gaps will fill with ink and you get gooey blobs on your final prints.

All of the Cloudy Collection prints work with just two colors. You can approximate gradients using halftones or cross-hatching, and you can print an entire plate with an ink mixed with a degree of transparency in it, but it takes some planning and some practice to get it all to work out right. Ultimately, you need to create one bitmap file for each layer of your print. The subsequent steps are a bit like magic to me, which is something I love. I simply send the digital file off to Syracuse, NY, and a few weeks later I get this glorious box of art!

···> *What about the environmental aspect? You seem to take great care to minimize the environmental impact of the entire printing process.*
Chemicals and volatile substances are common in printmaking, but it is really not that difficult to set up a shop that does not need all that junk. It just involves a few conscious decisions like buying recycled and sustainable paper stock, or using vegetable oil to clean up your ink. Boxcar run the print shop on 100% wind power, use vegetable-based inks, and print on sustainable bamboo paper custom-made by a German company. It may cost a little bit more here and there, but in a niche like fine-art letterpress printmaking, it is not going to make a huge dent in your bottom line.

···> *Have you noticed any increase in public awareness due to the rise of maker culture and platforms like etsy?*
Although the Cloudy Collection is only a year old at the time of writing, I have been watching and working on the web for about a decade. It is because of sites like etsy that I thought something like this might work. More specifically, the Tiny Showcase project run by Jon Buonaccorsi and Shea'la Finch in Providence, Rhode Island, was a model for making affordable, small-sized art and donating a portion of the proceeds to a good cause. I own more of their prints than I can count, so at some point I started thinking, "Hey, I can do this!"

The Cloudy Collection ⌁

THE SCARLET LETTERING · 2009 · ART PRINT
CLIENT The Cloudy Collection PRINTER Boxcar Press PRINTING Letterpress - Vandercook
From the Cloudy Collection, Volume I, Edition 3: "The Scarlet Lettering".
DESIGNER *David Huyck* (top)
DESIGNER *Linzie Hunter* (right)
DESIGNER *Nate Williams* (bottom left)
DESIGNER *Ray Fenwick* (bottom right)

TALK LESS DO MORE

DEAREST SWEETIE, WITH YOUR SOFT, BLACK EYELASHES & DELICATE LEGS I WATCH YOU AS YOU POINTEDLY TREAD, WITH YOUR WARM, TAN SKIN FLICKERING IN THE LIGHT, YOUR GENTLE MOVEMENTS ARE A DELIGHT TO SEE, OUTSIDE MY FENCE, AS YOU WALK LIGHTLY THROUGH THE GRASS. YOUR STEP SO SILENT AMONG THE BRITTLE BRANCHES AND LEAVES, I SOME-TIMES BARELY SEE YOU THERE GLIMPSING ONLY A SMALL RUSTLING IN THE DAPPLED LIGHT, BEFORE YOU LEAP AWAY INTO THE DARK FOREST.

The Cloudy Collection ⌁

THE SCARLET LETTERING · 2009 · ART PRINT
CLIENT The Cloudy Collection PRINTER Boxcar Press PRINTING Letterpress - Vandercook
From the Cloudy Collection, Volume I, Edition 3: "The Scarlet Lettering".
DESIGNER *Kate Bingaman-Burt* (top left)
DESIGNER *Marian Bantjes* (top right)
DESIGNER *Ray Frenden* (bottom)

HOVELS & HIDEAWAYS · 2009 · ART PRINT
CLIENT The Cloudy Collection PRINTER Boxcar Press PRINTING Letterpress - Vandercook
From the Cloudy Collection, Volume I, Edition 2: "Hovels & Hideaways".
DESIGNER *Vincent Stall* (top left)
DESIGNER *Scott Campbell* (bottom left)
DESIGNER *Bwana Spoons* (top right)
DESIGNER *Vera Brosgol* (middle right)
DESIGNER *David Huyck* (bottom right)

133|200   EC 08

Enormous Champion *

ALL GOOD THINGS · 2008 · ART PRINT *(top, bottom right)*
CLIENT Personal PRINTER Self-printed PRINTING Letterpress - Vandercook Universal I
Four-color letterpress print

MITTEN · 2008 · A-2 GREETING CARD *(bottom left)*
CLIENT Personal PRINTER Self-printed PRINTING Letterpress - Vandercook Universal I

A CETACEAN STUDY · 2009 · ART PRINT *(right page)*
CLIENT Personal PRINTER Self-printed PRINTING Letterpress - Vandercook Universal I
Seven-color letterpress print.

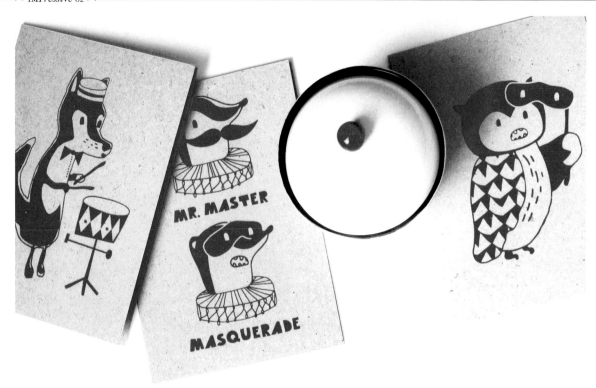

Darling Clementine ↝

MEET MONSIEUR MASQUERADE · 2008 · GREETING CARDS (top)
CLIENT Personal PRINTER Self-printed PRINTING Screen-print
The Meet Monsieur Masquerade series is inspired by quirky circus animals and French clichés.
The cards are Screen-print by hand using strong colours on environmentally- friendly paper.

PARIS! SERIES · 2009 · GREETING CARDS (bottom, 2 images)
CLIENT Ourselves PRINTER Feburman PRINTING Offset
The Paris! series is a collection of 12 designs that all celebrate the French language in all its glory.

House Industries ⌁

MAPLE B · 2009 · ART *(top)*
PHOTO-LETTERING PLINC ALPHABET BLOCK · 2009 · ART *(top right)*
PHOTO-LETTERING NEUTRA SLAB ALPHABET BLOCK · 2009 · ART *(middle left & right)*
ALEXANDER GIRARD BLOCK · 2009 · ART *(bottom left)*
MAPLE BLOCKS · 2009 · ART *(bottom right)*
CLIENT Personal PRINTER David Dodde PRINTING Screen-print
House Industries maple block prints.

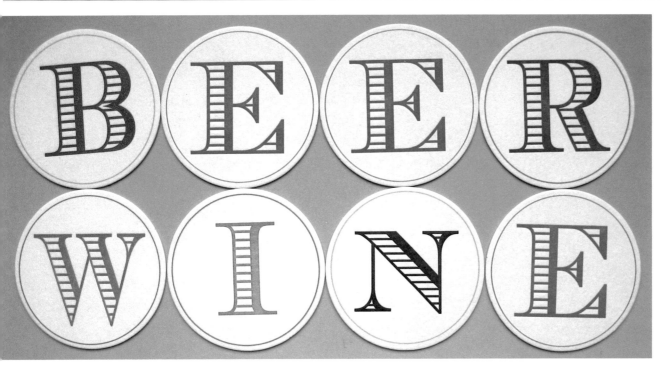

coasters spell **COCKTAIL**

Sesame Letterpress ˄

LETTERS · 2009 · COASTERS *(top, 3 images)*
SNOWFLAKE · 2009 · COASTER *(left)*
POLAR BEAR · 2009 · COASTER *(bottom)*
CLIENT Personal PRINTER Selfprinted PRINTING Letterpress

DESIGN (ALL) *Breck Hostetter*

Lunalux ⌐

THE ORANGE ICECREAMS · 2009 · RETAIL SIGNAGE *(top left)*
CLIENT Izzy's Ice Cream PRINTER Lunalux PRINTING Letterpress - Vandercook
Printed with vintage wood type.

COTTON CANDY ICECREAM SIGN · 2009 · RETAIL SIGNAGE *(top right)*
CLIENT Izzy's Ice Cream PRINTER Lunalux PRINTING Vandercook
antique wood type, opaque pink ink.

ICE CREAM DOTS - THE FIRST 27 · 2009 · RETAIL SIGNAGE *(bottom left)*
CLIENT Izzy's Ice Cream PRINTER Lunalux PRINTING Vandercook
First 27 ice-cream signs, in a series of 150+ - each set with antique wood and lead type, printed in a
limited edition of seven per dot.

LEMON SORBET · 2009 · RETAIL SIGNAGE *(bottom right)*
CLIENT Izzy's Ice Cream PRINTER Lunalux PRINTING Vandercook

Letteria ⌁

WOODEN LETTERS · 2008 *(top)*
CLIENT Personal PRINTER Letteria PRINTING Letterpress

LA VIE EN ROSE · 2009 · COASTERS *(left)*
CLIENT Personal PRINTER Letteria PRINTING Letterpress

BIRD · 2008 · GIFTTAG *(bottom left)*
CLIENT Personal PRINTER Letteria PRINTING Letterpress

HEART · 2008 *(bottom right)*
CLIENT Personal PRINTER Letteria PRINTING Letterpress

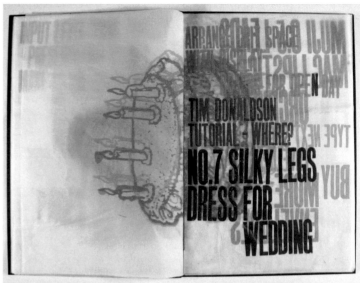

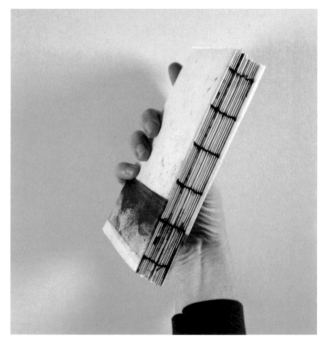

Philippa Wood ↝

ANNOY BRIAN · 2009 · UNIQUE ARTISTS' BOOK *(top left)*
CLIENT Personal PRINTER Self-printed PRINTING Letterpress, typewriter.
A 10 m long book. Concertina folded then bound to an outer casing.

DONE · 2009 · ARTISTS' BOOK *(top right, middle left)*
CLIENT Personal PRINTER Self-printed PRINTING Screen-print, letterpress.
Produced as a call for entries submission to an exhibition entitled Closure.

UNTITLED · 2008 · UNIQUE ARTISTS' BOOK *(middle right)*
CLIENT Personal PRINTER Self-printed PRINTING Etching press
Spine detail of coptic bound book produced from the printed waste tissue paper from the etching press.

PERSONAL SPACES 1 - HOUSE AND HOME · 2006 · ARTISTS' BOOK *(bottom left)*
CLIENT Personal PRINTER Self-printed PRINTING Screen-print

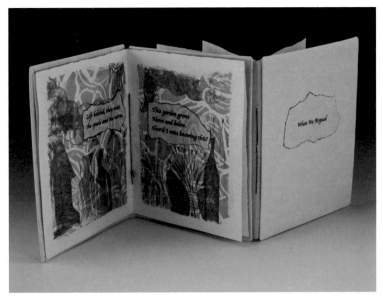

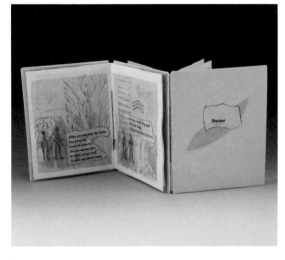

Alicia Griswold ⌁

IN THE GARDEN · 2009 · DOS-A-DOS *(top left, middle right)*
CLIENT Personal PRINTER Self-printed PRINTING Rubber stamps
Handmade and hand printed with hand-carved rubber stamps, collaged text, two prose poems
"Ancient" and "When We Argued" by artist. 16 pages, 4 x 5 inches closed..

HOW TO DISTINGUISH SCENTS · 2009 · ACCORDION BOOK *(top right, middle left, bottom)*
CLIENT Personal PRINTER Atlanta Printmakers Studio PRINTING Solar plates
16 pages, all text and images created with solar plates.

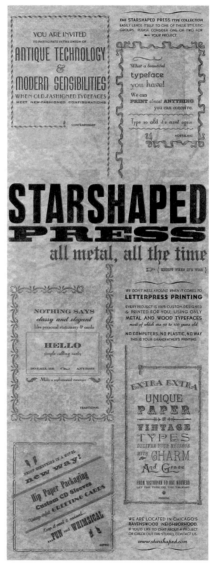

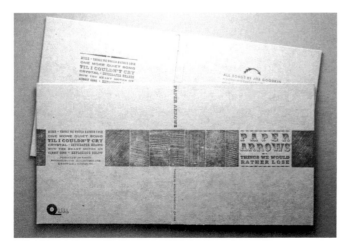

Starshaped Press ·

STARSHAPED PRESS PROMOTIONAL MAILER · 2009 · POSTER *(top, 2 images)*
CLIENT Personal PRINTER Self-printed PRINTING Letterpress - Vandercook SP 15
Printed as a promotional piece for prospective clients. This poster outlines the principals we uphold
and showcases samples of the complicated metal and wood type setting that we do.

PAPER ARROWS · 2009 · CD SLEEVE *(bottom)*
Client Paper Arrows Printer Selfprinted Printing Letterpress - Chandler + Price 10x15
We set all of the metal type by hand (many different typefaces), and the wood pattern is created by
printing the back sides of wood type.

DESIGNER (ALL) *Jennifer Farrell*

Starshaped Press ✴

IN HARD TIMES, YOU'RE GOOD PEOPLE · 2009 · POSTER *(top left)*
DO IT YOURSELF BROADSIDE · 2009 · POSTER *(top right)*
WE'RE IN THIS TOGETHER · 2009 · POSTER *(middle left)*
CLIENT Personal PRINTER Self-printed PRINTING Letterpress - Vandercook SP-15
1 of 3 broadsides in our Hard Times series of LP-sized prints.
DESIGNER *Jennifer Farrell*

URBAN GARDENING · 2009 · POSTER *(right)*
CLIENT Personal PRINTER Self-printed PRINTING Letterpress - Vandercook SP-15
This poster was created for the Bridgeport WPA poster show in Chicago in spring 2009. It is the
first in a series of WPA-inspired posters.
DESIGNER *Jennifer Farrell*

Something Wonderful Design ·

HOME SWEET HOME (EDITION 23/24) · 2009 · ART PRINT *(top left)*
CLIENT Personal PRINTER Self-printed PRINTING Linoprint
Editioned linoprint from two original linocuts, designed to commission.

LOVE · 2009 · ART PRINT *(top)*
CLIENT Personal PRINTER Self-printed PRINTING Linoprint
Hand-printed from an original design cut into lino, onto painted canvas on a stretcher.

A-Z: ALPHABET IN A BLUE SKY · 2009 · ART PRINT *(bottom left)*
CLIENT Personal PRINTER Self-printed PRINTING Linoprint
Hand-printed from individual linoblocks onto canvas.

ITALIAN GOTHIC ALPHABET · 2009 · ART PRINT *(bottom right)*
CLIENT Personal PRINTER Self-printed PRINTING Linoprint
An editioned and hand-printed linoprint made to an original design, with lettering taken from an

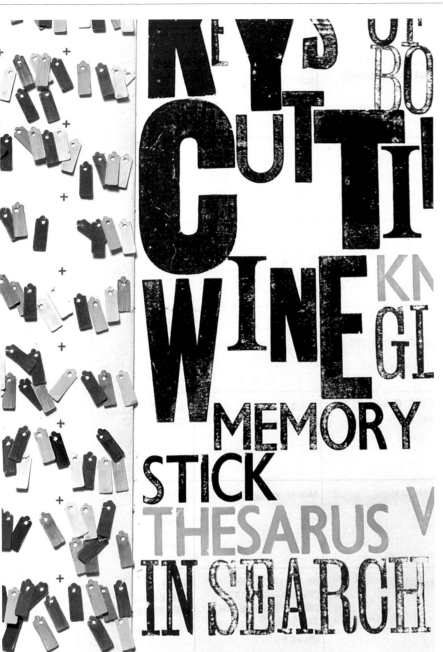

Philippa Wood ⌁

RESPONSE · 2008 · ARTISTS' BOOK *(top, 2 images)*
CLIENT Personal PRINTER Self-printed

HOBNOBS TO EARRINGS · 2009 · UNIQUE ARTISTS' BOOK *(bottom)*
CLIENT Personal PRINTER Self-printed

General Pattern ⚓

PURVEYORS · 2008 · POSTER *(top)*
CLIENT Personal PRINTER Self-printed PRINTING Letterpress - Stephenson Blake Proofing Press

MAGIC · 2009 · POSTER *(top right)*
CLIENT Personal PRINTER Self-printed PRINTING Letterpress - Stephenson Blake Proofing Press

WINTERLUDE · 2009 · POSTER *(right)*
CLIENT The Betsey Trotwood PRINTER Self-printed PRINTING Screen-print

VENETIAS · 2009 · POSTER *(right page)*
CLIENT Venetias Coffee Shop PRINTER Self-printed PRINTING Screen-print

DESIGNER (ALL) *James Brown*

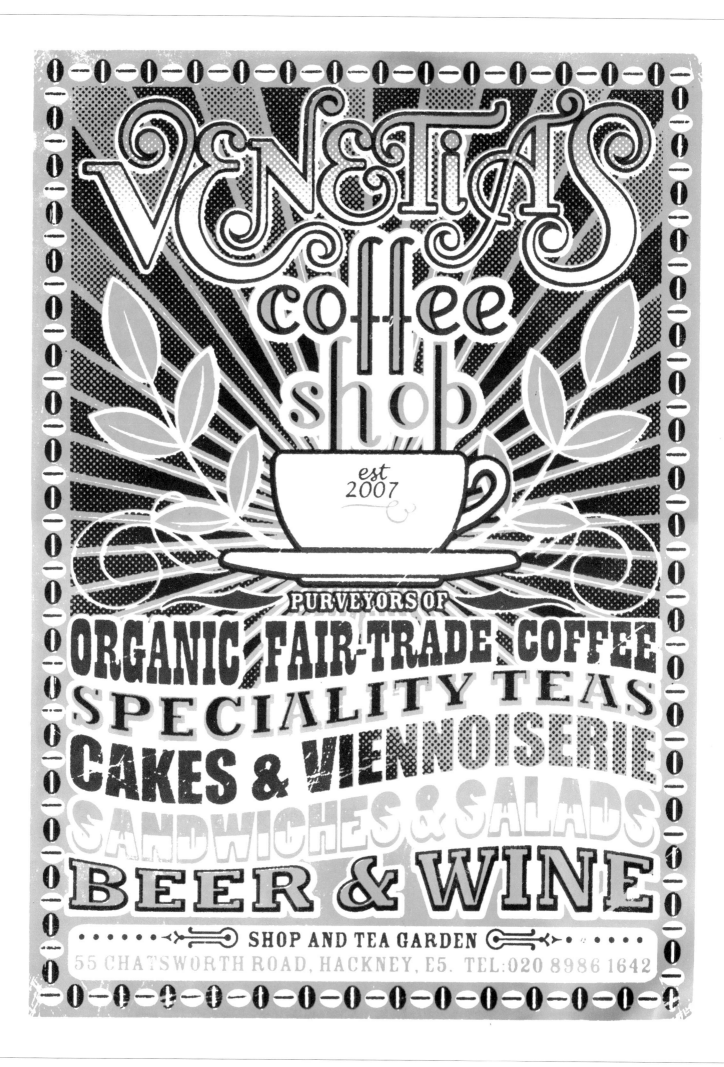

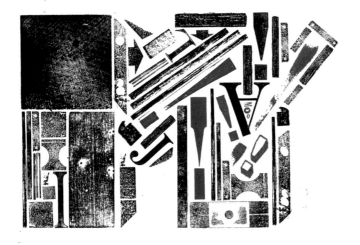

Craig Ward ↝

ALPHABET CITY 002 // LONDON · 2007 · POSTER / PRINT *(top)*
CLIENT Personal PRINTER Self-printed PRINTING Letterpress - Adana 5x3

MTV LOGO TREATMENT · 2007 · LOGO *(left)*
CLIENT MTV PRINTER Self-printed PRINTING Letterpress - Adana 5x3

GIMME SHELTER · 2008 · BOOK COVER PROPOSAL *(right page, top left)*
CLIENT Simon & Schuster - New York PRINTER Self-printed PRINTING Letterpress - Adana 5x3

ALPHABET CITY 001 // NEW YORK · 2007 · POSTER / PRINT *(right page, top right)*
CLIENT Personal PRINTER Self-printed PRINTING Letterpress - Adana 5x3

LEARNING AMERICAN · 2007 · ILLUSTRATION FOR MAGAZINE *(right page, bottom left)*
CLIENT New York Times Saturday Magazine PRINTER Self-printed PRINTING Letterpress - Adana 5x3

F2 Design

WOVENHAND · 2009 · POSTER *(right page, bottom right)*
CLIENT Allan Brown PRINTER Self-printed PRINTING Letterpress - Proof press
DESIGNER *Dirk Fowler*

GIMME
SHELTER

MARY ELIZABETH WILLIAMS

TRUE TALES FROM THE BUBBLE

UPPER WEST SIDE
CENTRAL PARK
UPPER EAST "„SiDE
ROOSEVELT ISLA
MID TOWN
MIDTOWN EAST
MURRAY
WeST hiLL
ChELSEA GRaMMErcY
GREEN [EAST]
WiCh VILLAGE
SOhO LOWER
TRIBECA! CHInATOWN EAST SIDE
FiNaNCIAL DISTRICT

LEaRNiNG AMEricaN

ONE WOLF
90% DEATH SEX
FRIDAY, MARCH 6
BASH'S no. 2

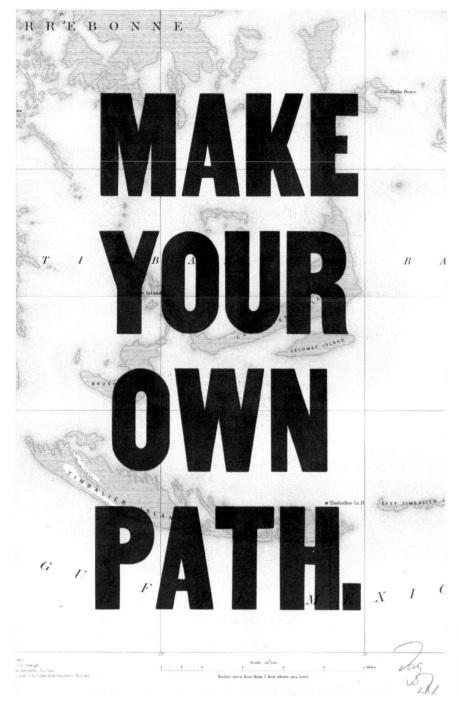

Douglas Wilson ⌁

MAKE YOUR OWN PATH · 2007 · POSTER *(top left)*
CLIENT Personal PRINTER The Scarlet Letterpress PRINTING Letterpress - Vandercook #4
Printed on antique maps.

MAKE YOUR OWN PATH ALTERNATE · 2007 · POSTER *(bottom left)*
CLIENT Personal PRINTER The Scarlet Letterpress PRINTING Letterpress - Vandercook #4
Alternate poster printed on antique maps.

GET LOST · 2008 · POSTER *(bottom right)*
CLIENT Personal PRINTER The Scarlet Letterpress PRINTING Letterpress - Vandercook #4
Printed on antique maps.

Ophelia Chong ⌁

CALL ME / EAT ME · 2008 · PAINT CHIP CARDS *(top right)*
CLIENT Personal PRINTER Self-printed PRINTING Letterpress - Vandercook
Wood type printed on paint sample cards.

MEWI ITHOU TYOU

JUNE.29...OUTLAND.BALLROOM...7PM...WITH
MAKE.BELIEVE,VEDA,BUSINESS/CASULTY

Hand Letterpressed by Douglas Wilson   douglasiswilson@hotmail.com

NPR

and

All Things Considered

present:

SOUND CLIPS!

An Exploration of the Unusual and Exciting in Audible Form

Printed using antique wood and metal type on a 1949 Vandercook No.4 Proof Press

Hand Letterpressed by Douglas Wilson .... douglasiswilson@hotmail.com

DO WHAT YOU LOVE, LOVE WHAT YOU DO.

Douglas Wilson

MEWITHOUTYOU · 2006 · CONCERT POSTER *(top left)*
CLIENT Personal PRINTER The Scarlet Letterpress PRINTING Letterpress - Vandercook #4

NPR SOUND CLIPS · 2007 · POSTER *(top middle)*
CLIENT National Public Radio PRINTER The Scarlet Letterpress PRINTING Letterpress - Vandercook #4

DO WHAT YOU LOVE, LOVE WHAT YOU DO. · 2009 · POSTER *(top right)*
CLIENT Personal PRINTER The Scarlet Letterpress PRINTING Letterpress - Vandercook #4

WHEN LIFE GIVES YOU LEMONS, MAKE LEMONADE · 2009 · POSTER *(bottom left)*
CLIENT Personal PRINTER The Scarlet Letterpress PRINTING Letterpress - Vandercook #4

KEEP IT SIMPLE STUPID · 2007 · LETTERPRESSED POSTER *(bottom right)*
CLIENT Personal PRINTER The Scarlet Letterpress PRINTING Letterpress - Vandercook #4

WHEN LIFE GIVES YOU LEMONS, MAKE LEMONADE!

KEEP IT SIMPLE STUPID.

MIKE & AMY FINDERS BAND

▷ Opening Show ◁

Shades of Bluegrass

$12 FRIDAY, MARCH 23, 7:30

THE LISTENING ROOM

Knights of Pythias Hall, 106 N. Denver   Hastings, NE
Students: $8   Call 402-463-6248 for Information
Poster by Bennett Holzworth

STORYHILL

★ Opening Show ★
Emily Dunbar
$12   FRIDAY, MAY 4, 7:30
THE LISTENING ROOM

Knights of Pythias Hall, 106 N. Denver   Hastings, NE
Students: $8   Call 402-463-6248 for Information
Poster by Bennett Holzworth

Type B Press ⤳

LISTENING ROOM SEASON SERIES · 2007 · POSTER (*4 images*)
CLIENT The Listening Room PRINTER Type B Press PRINTING Letterpress - Vandercook SP 15
These posters were printed for a series of folk music concerts that the Listening Room hosts. The images were printed from pixel-like wood matrix that friend and carpenter extraordinaire Jack Sandeen created for me.

JALAN
CROSSLAND

▶ Opening Show ◀
Todd Brown
$12 SATURDAY, FEBRUARY 17, 7:30
THE LISTENING ROOM

Knights of Pythias Hall, 106 N. Denver   Hastings, NE
Students: $8   Call 402-463-6248 for Information
Poster by Bennett Holzworth

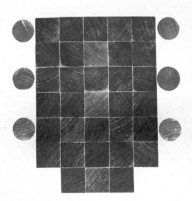

JEFFREY
FOUCAULT

● Opening Show ●
Peter Lainson
$12   FRIDAY, MARCH 9, 7:30
THE LISTENING ROOM

Knights of Pythias Hall, 106 N. Denver   Hastings, NE
Students: $8   Call 402-463-6248 for Information
Poster by Bennett Holzworth

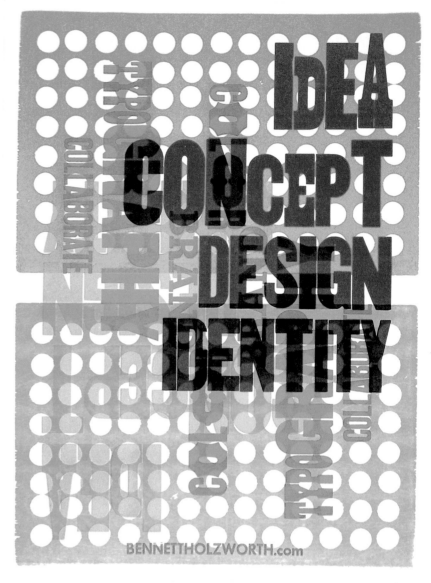

Type B Press ✦

MARK ERELLI LISTENING ROOM · 2006 · POSTER *(top left)*
CLIENT Mark Erelli PRINTER Self-printed PRINTING Letterpress - Vandercook SP 15
The large linoleum cut directly references Mark Erelli's song "Imaginary Wars" about a pine forest
that was replaced by a housing development when he was a child.
LINOLEUM CUTS *Suzanne Holzworth, Bennett Holzworth*

SELF PROMO · 2006 · POSTER *(top right)*
CLIENT Personal PRINTER Type B Press PRINTING Letterpress - Vandercook SP 15
Five-color self-promo poster that was printed from drilled recycled plywood, wood and metal type.

JOHN VANDERSLICE · 2009 · POSTER *(bottom left)*
CLIENT One Percent Productions PRINTER Self-printed PRINTING Letterpress - 12x18 Chandler & Price
The ornamentation in the poster was printed from paper doilies that were glued five-high, varnished
and mounted to be type-high. Instead of cutting a block or making a plate, I used existing paper
doilies from the local craft store. The blue/green portion of the poster was also stackled and mounted
paper doilies that then had the illustration cut into them. The limted budget of this poster required the use of inexpensive materials. The use of mundane everyday things (paper doilies) to
make something beautiful and artistic was the perfect fit for John Vanerslice's music.

MARK ERELLI · 2008 · POSTER *(bottom right)*
CLIENT Mark Erelli PRINTER Self-printed PRINTING Letterpress - Vandercook SP 15
Commissioned letterpress poster for Mark Erelli's die-hard fans who supported Mark's upcoming
album "Delivered", through the "Barn Raising" effort. These were letterpress printed from a mix
of handset wood and metal type, hand-carved plywood, hand-carved linoleum and one metal block.
Mark's folk music was a perfect fit for hand-printed letterpress.
WOOD AND LINOLEUM CUTS *Suzanne Holzworth and Bennett Holzworth*

SlowPrint Letterpress Studios ⚲

IGOR KOPELNITSKY · 2009 · CARD SET *(top left, bottom left)*
CLIENT Sparked.biz PRINTER Self-printed PRINTING Letterpress - Heidelberg 10x15 Windmill
ILLUSTRATION *Kopelnitsky* DESIGN *Sparked.biz, SlowPrint*

RUDOLF KOCH QUOTE · 1990 · ART PRINT *(top upper right)*
CLIENT Personal PRINTER Self-printed PRINTING Letterpress - Vandercook Universal I
Rudolf Koch Quote with specimen of Hermann Zapf's Optima - handset foundry type, three colors
on dampened Stonehenge paper.
DESIGN *Peter Fraterdeus*

LETTERS MINGLE SOULS · 2008 · NOTE CARD *(top lower right)*
CLIENT Personal PRINTER Self-printed PRINTING Letterpress - Vandercook Universal I
Quote from John Donne (17th C).
DESIGN & LETTERING *Peter Fraterdeus*

SlowPrint Letterpress Studios ❧

SLOWPRINT STUDIO · 2009 · BUSINESS CARD *(top left)*
CLIENT Personal   PRINTER Self-printed   PRINTING Letterpress - Heidelberg 10x15 Windmill
DESIGN *Peter Fraterdeus*

AMOR OMNIA VINCIT (LOVE CONQUERS ALL) · 2009 · NOTE CARD *(top right)*
CLIENT Personal   PRINTER Self-printed   PRINTING Letterpress - Heidelberg 10x15 Windmill
DESIGN & LETTERING *Peter Fraterdeus*

LOVE · 2008 · NOTE CARD *(bottom left)*
CLIENT Personal   PRINTER Self-printed   PRINTING Letterpress - Heidelberg 10x15 Windmill
DESIGN & LETTERING *Peter Fraterdeus*

LOVE IS AN ENDLESS MYSTERY FOR IT HAS NOTHING ELSE TO EXPLAIN IT. ·
2008 · ART PRINT *(bottom right)*
CLIENT Personal   PRINTER Self-printed   PRINTING Letterpress - Vandercook 219
Quote of Rabindranth Tagore. Handset 19th C wood type, photopolymer, and foundry type. Three transparent colors.
DESIGN *Peter Fraterdeus*

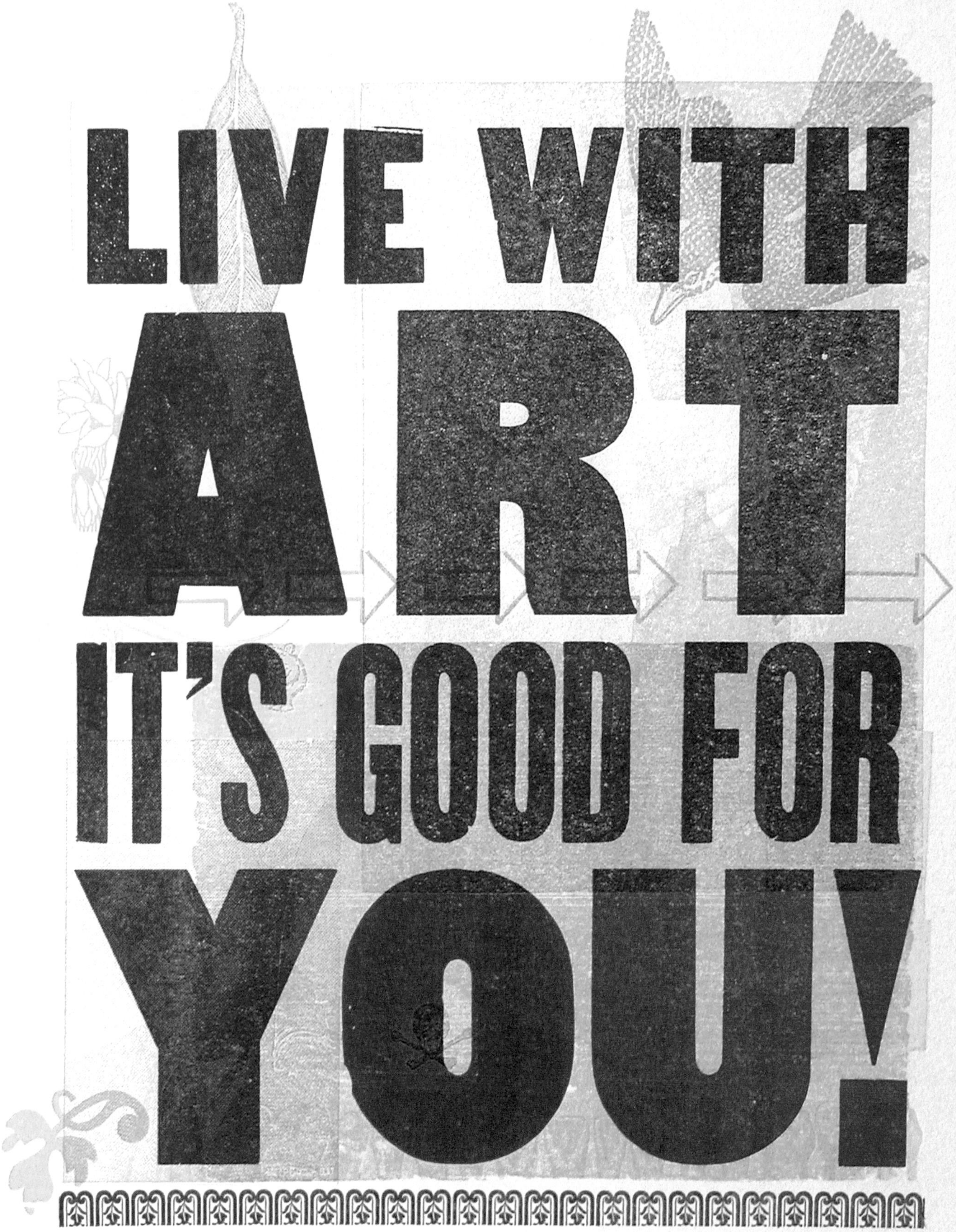
LIVE WITH
ART
IT'S GOOD FOR
YOU!

Mike Burton ᴕ

LIVE WITH ART (SMALL SIZE) · 2008 · ART PRINT *(left page)*
CLIENT Jen Bekman for 20x200 PRINTER Cranky Pressman PRINTING Letterpress - Original Heidelberg
Letterpress interpretation of Jen Bekman's slogan "Live with art, It's good for you!" Art print
produced exclusively for 20x200. Created entirely from antique wood type and ornaments. Four-
color letterpress.

BLOODSHOT RECORDS BEER-B-Q'S POSTER · 2009 · POSTER *(top left)*
CLIENT Bloodshot Records PRINTER Lucky Bunny PRINTING Screen-print
Commemorative poster for Bloodshot Records 15 year anniversary summer BBQ parties. Two-
color screen-print. All proceeds of the poster go to Common Threads, a Chicago-based charity that
teaches low-income children how to cook wholesome and affordable meals.

LIVE WITH ART (MEDIUM SIZE) · 2008 · POSTER *(top right)*
CLIENT Jen Bekman for 20x200 PRINTER Cranky Pressman PRINTING Letterpress - Original Heidelberg
Letterpress interpretation of Jen Bekman's slogan "Live with art, It's good for you!" Art print produced exclusively for 20x200. Created mostly from antique wood type and ornaments. Line work
illustrations by Joey Parlett. Six-color print plus one blind embossment.

LIVE WITH ART LARGE · 2008 · POSTER *(bottom left)*
CLIENT Jen Bekman for 20x200 PRINTER Cranky Pressman PRINTING Letterpress - Vandercook
Letterpress interpretation of Jen Bekman's slogan "Live with art, It's good for you!" Art print produced exclusively for 20x200. Created entirely from antique wood type and ornaments. Two-color
print, hand-brayered ink.

PROCEED AND BE BOLD! · 2008 · POSTCARD *(bottom right)*
CLIENT Brown Finch Films PRINTER Cranky Pressman PRINTING Letterpress - Original Heidelberg
Postcard for documentary about letterpress printer Amos Paul Kennedy Jr. produced by Brown
Finch Films. Collaboration with the Cranky Pressman. I can't take credit for the concept, but I'm
really excited about the gradient. Three/one-color letterpress, made entirely from antique wood and
lead type.

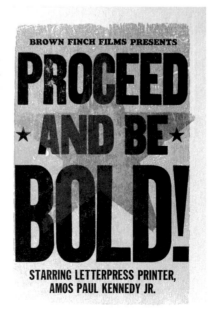

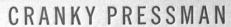

Mike Burton ᴧ

CRANKY PRESSMAN 09 · 2008 · CALENDAR *(top, 2 images)*
CLIENT Cranky Pressman PRINTER Cranky Pressman PRINTING Letterpress - Original Heidelberg
Scary and ugly looking just like the upcoming year. The Cranky Pressman 2009 Calendar is a fitting
tribute to what likely will prove to be a very crappy year. Three-color letterpress. 2 magnesium plates
for the bear illustration, antique wood type for the 09, and authentic hot type for the smaller info.
ART DIRECTOR *Jamie Berger*

JUDE INTERIORS · 2008 · BUSINESS CARD *(bottom, 2 images)*
CLIENT Cranky Pressman PRINTER Cranky Pressman PRINTING Letterpress - Original Heidelberg
Created entirely from authentic hot type.

DANIELSON POSTER · 2006 · POSTER *(right page)*
CLIENT Beachland Ballroom PRINTER Mikey Burton PRINTING Letterpress - Vandercook Universal I
Poster for show at the Beachland Ballroom in Cleveland, OH, five-color letterpress. Created entirely
from antique wood type and ornaments. Work done for Little Jacket.

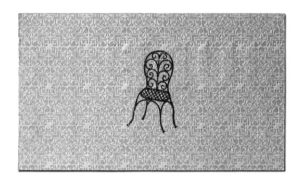

OH NO!

CLEVE LAND

BEACH LAND

OHIO

PAN ON

With The X Bolex 9pm 7.27.06 $10

67898   X

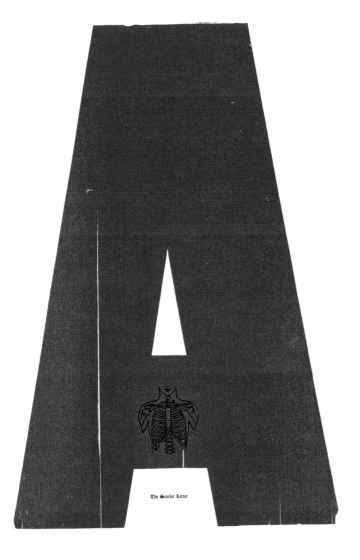

Douglas Wilson ~

THE SCARLET LETTER · 2005 · POSTER *(top left)*
CLIENT Personal PRINTER The Scarlet Letterpress PRINTING Letterpress - Vandercook 325G
Printed from the type collection of John Horn.

Ophelia Chong ~

BEHAVE · 2008 · PATCH *(top right)*
CLIENT Personal PRINTER Self-printed PRINTING Letterpress - Vandercook
Wood block type with linocut block-cut of a target.

YES / NO · 2008 · PATCH *(bottom left)*
CLIENT Personal PRINTER Self-printed PRINTING Letterpress - Vandercook
"Yes No" printed on canvas. Target is a linocut block print.

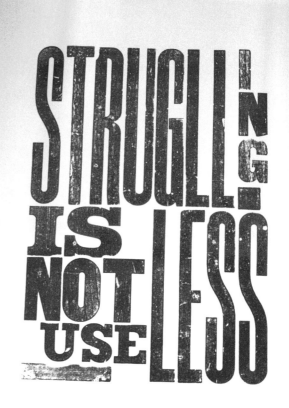

Armina Ghazaryan ∿

MOVIE POSTER · 2009 · POSTER *(top right)*
CLIENT MIAT museum, Ghent, Belgium PRINTER MIAT PRINTING Letterpress
Limited edition of 100.

MOVIE POSTER · 2009 · POSTER *(top right, bottom left)*
CLIENT Personal PRINTING Letterpress

STRUGLING IS NOT USELESS · 2008 · POSTER *(bottom right)*
CLIENT Personal PRINTING Letterpress

Ophelia Chong ๑

WALKING IN XO · 2009 · POSTER *(top left)*
LOVE AND ROCKETS · 2009 · POSTER *(top right)*
BANGPOWBANG - FEMALE TROUBLE · 2009 · POSTER *(bottom left)*
BANGPOWBANG - AMERICA GETS TOUCH · 2009 · POSTER *(bottom right)*
CLIENT Personal PRINTER Self-printed PRINTING Letterpress - Vandercook 320G Hand Proof Press
Found ephemera hand-printed. Wood-block type with yellow and warm red inks.

Ophelia Chong ⌁

FLYING XO MAN · 2009 · POSTER *(top left)*
YOUR FEAR · 2008 · POSTER *(top right)*
XO EUPHORIA · 2009 · POSTER *(bottom left)*
JOY OF XO · 2009 · POSTER *(bottom middle)*
TWO SIDES OF XO · 2009 · POSTER *(bottom right)*
CLIENT Personal PRINTER Self-printed PRINTING Letterpress - Vandercook 320G Hand Proof Press
Found ephemera hand printed. Hand-set wood block type and warm red inks.

Een constructief jaar gewenst.
Je vous souhaite une année constructive.
Wishing you a constructive new year.
Stéphane de Schrevel

Een constructief jaar gewenst.
Je vous souhaite une année constructive.
Wishing you a constructive new year.
Stéphane de Schrevel

Stéphane de Schrevel ↝

SEASON'S WISHES · 2009 · GREETING CARDS *(top left)*
CLIENT Personal PRINTER Kamer 108, Gent PRINTING Letterpress - FAG Control 405 flatbed cylinder proof press

ZIN IN LETTEREN · 2008 · BOOKLET COVER *(top right)*
CLIENT Vlaams Fonds voor de Letteren, MIAT, Gent PRINTER Kamer 108, Gent PRINTING Letterpress - FAG Control 405 flatbed cylinder proof press

SEASON'S WISHES · 2008 · GREETING CARDS *(middle left, bottom left)*
CLIENT Personal PRINTER Kamer 108, Gent PRINTING Letterpress - FAG Control 405 flatbed cylinder proof press

BIRTH ANNOUNCEMENT · 2009 · CARDS *(middle right, 3 images of 4)*
CLIENT Karin Van Eygen & Edwin Koster PRINTER Kamer 108, Gent PRINTING Letterpress - FAG Control 405 flatbed cylinder proof press

www.typejamming.com

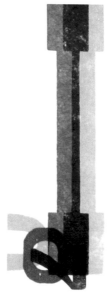

www.typejamming.com

www.typejamming.com

www.typejamming.com

Stéphane de Schrevel ↝

SEASON'S WISHES · 2007 · GREETING CARDS *(top left)*
CLIENT Personal PRINTER Kamer 108, Gent PRINTING Letterpress - FAG Control 405 flatbed cylinder proof press

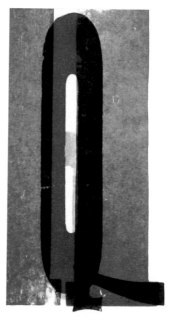

www.typejamming.com

The Caseroom Press ᴥ

DANTE - THE INFERNO • BOOK ILLUSTRATIONS:
| CANTO XXVI: THE COUNSELLORS OF FRAUD · 1991 *(top left)*
| CANTO XX: THE SORCERERS · 2009 *(bottom left)*
| CANTO XIX: THE SIMONIACS · 2009 *(right)*
| CANTO XVIII: THE FLATTERERS, PLUNGED IN FILTH · 1991 *(right page, top left)*
| CANTO XXIII: THE HYPOCRITES IN THEIR GILDED CLOAKS · 1990 *(r. page, top right)*
| CANTO XXXII: THE FROZEN LAKE OF COCYTUS · 2001 *(right page, bottom left)*
| CANTO IV: THE VIRTUOUS PAGANS • 1990 *(right page, top right)*
CLIENT Personal PRINTER Self-printed PRINTING Letterpress - Vandercook

DESIGNER *Barrie Tullett*

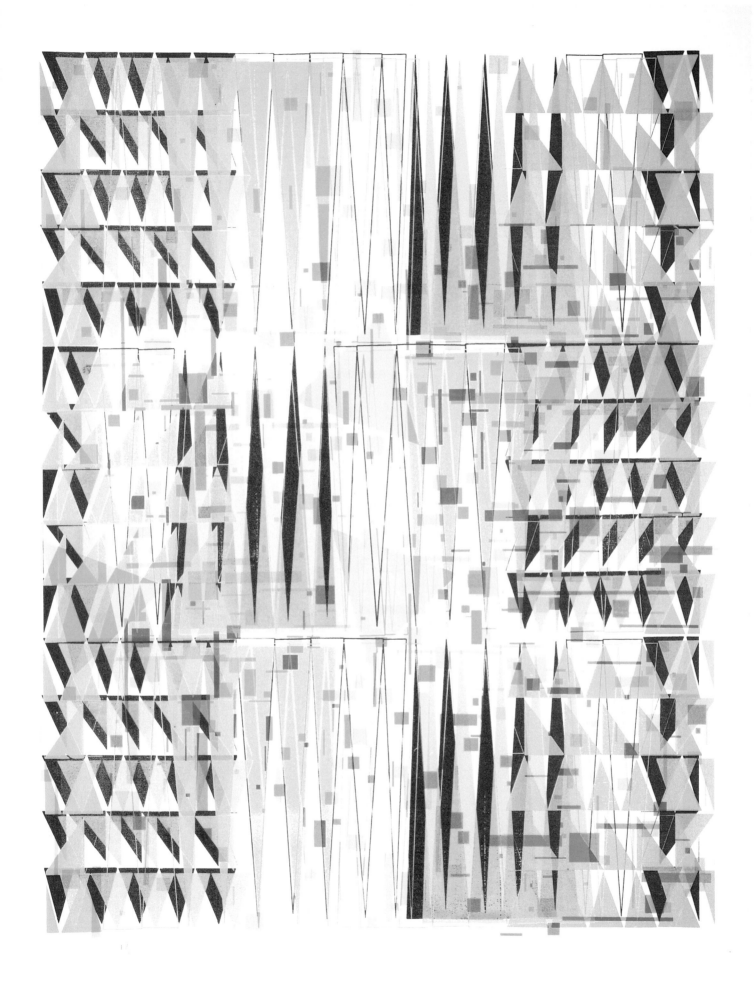

Kate Gibb ∿

MONOGRAPH 1, 2, 4, 5, 9 · 2008 · ART PRINTS *(left & right page, 5 images)*
CLIENT Personal PRINTER Self-printed PRINTING Screen-print

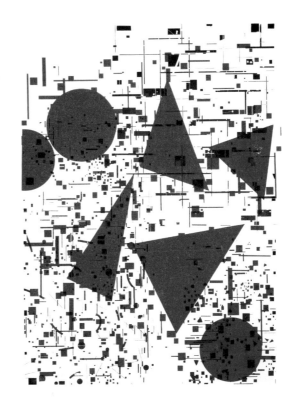

Dumbo feather,

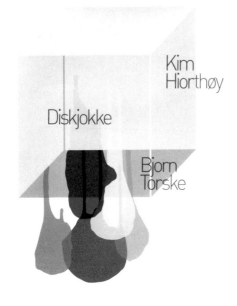

Kim
Hiorthøy

Diskjokke

Bjorn
Torske

Smalltown Supersound
showcase

Saturday March 15 08

pass it on.

Sonnenzimmer ↝

TAQWACORE · 2008 · POSTER *(top left)*
CLIENT Homeroom PRINTER Self-printed PRINTING Screen-print - American Tempo
DESIGNER *Nick Butcher, Nadine Nakanishi*

SMALLTOWN SUPERSOUND · 2008 · POSTER *(top right)*
CLIENT The Empty Bottle PRINTER Self-printed PRINTING Screen-print - American Tempo
DESIGNER *Nick Butcher, Nadine Nakanishi*

WHEN WORDS MEET IMAGE · 2009 · POSTER *(bottom left)*
CLIENT Columbia College Chicago PRINTER Self-printed PRINTING Screen-print - American Tempo
DESIGNER *Nick Butcher, Nadine Nakanishi*

DUMBOFEATHER · 2008 · POSTER *(bottom right)*
CLIENT Dumbofeather PRINTER Self-printed PRINTING Screen-print - Cincinatti flatbed press
DESIGNER *Nadine Nakanishi*

When Words Meet Images

TAQ
WA
CO
RE

Riz MC
All Natural
Al Thawra

CANYONS OF STATIC

Sonnenzimmer ⌁

THE WALKMEN · 2009 · POSTER *(top left)*
CLIENT The Metro PRINTER Self-printed PRINTING Screen-print - American Tempo
DESIGNER *Nick Butcher, Nadine Nakanishi*

A HAWK AND A HACKSAW | DAMON AND NAOMI · 2009 · POSTER *(top right)*
CLIENT A Hawk And A Hacksaw | Damon and Naomi PRINTER Self-printed PRINTING Screen-print - American Tempo
DESIGNER *Nick Butcher, Nadine Nakanishi*

CANYONS OF STATIC · 2009 · POSTER *(bottom left)*
CLIENT Canyons of Static PRINTER Self-printed PRINTING Screen-print - American Tempo
DESIGNER *Nick Butcher, Nadine Nakanishi*

DEAD C · 2008 · POSTER *(bottom right)*
CLIENT The Empty Bottle PRINTER Self-printed PRINTING Screen-print - American Tempo
DESIGNER *Nick Butcher*

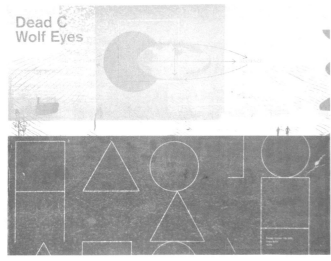

Dead C
Wolf Eyes

A
HAWK
AND
A
HACKSAW

DAMON
&
NAOMI

FALL
2009
NORTH AMERICA

Faile •/•

Not everything is black and white in the world of Faile, but they do love their binaries – and a touch of controversy. Brooklyn-based street art pioneers Patrick McNeill and Patrick Miller have worked together for a good 17 years: according to legend, they met on the first day of high school, trading fireworks. With bold motifs, yet a light, precise, and hand-crafted touch, the—still-mischievous—duo infernale takes a page or two out of comics, pulp fiction, and mainstream art culture to take the graphic novel back to the streets. Mixing and matching prints, paintings, wood, and murals, they stage their own visual interventions to inscribe cityscapes and gallery walls between London, New York, and Bethlehem with their trademark stark narrative. The result is urban poetry in motion: playful, saucy, amusing, jarring, and sometimes plain absurd.

···> *You are well-known for your printed urban interventions—often spilling over into the art realm. But let's return to the beginning: How did you learn the tricks of the trade?*

Although we studied graphic design in art school, the majority of our time was spent hijacking our school's screen-printing rooms. Thanks to the clandestine support of a few helpful teachers, we managed to take the printing class almost every semester. Looking back, I think we got to where we are today by putting in a lot of late nights and following up on every opportunity—plus creating a few of our own on the way.

···> *If you had to explain the screen-printing process to a novice—what are the particular advantages and drawbacks? Anything a beginner should know?*

The immediacy of printing and the anticipation of that final pull is a great attribute of printing. It is a medium that embraces mistakes and allows for experimentation. So, watch that squeegee angle, save your scraps and always be open to the process! It is a time-consuming process, but it really depends on the number of editions and amount of layers you are planning to do. Mono-printing has always been our main interest, so we do a lot of that. Fortunately for us, this particular technique is a little bit more forgiving than editions. And so far, we have been very fortunate to see our ideas come to fruition. I suppose where there is a will, there is a way.

So, we do not see many drawbacks with screen-printing, other than the laborious screen creation process and the required wait—there is simply not enough time in the day to do everything that you want to do.

···> *So, in order to make the most of your time and attention, how do you pick your projects and topics?*

You know, ideas come to you and you follow them. Sometimes they take you somewhere, other times they lead to something else. It is all about being open and receptive. We like motifs that tell a story, this has always been central to our thinking—whether that story plays out in one image or across an entire show.

···> *Considering your choice of motifs and artistic juxtapositions, what is your position on the general (and age-old) debate on the merit of reproduction in art? Is the distinction between copy and original even relevant anymore?*

We do not think so. The only kind of reproduction we are concerned about is the unauthorized kind.

···> *With digital networks facilitating access to information and creative tools, have you noticed any change in the public perception of urban art or handmade prints over the last few years?*

Although the computer is an important tool in our process, we have always been interested in the handmade aspect of the work. I think the internet has made all the work that much more accessible and this is the biggest change we have seen in terms of the digital side. It has totally changed the way artists can release work and make it accessible to potential collectors.

···> *So, what adds that special, covetable touch to your own art prints?*

The Faile Secret Sauce and plenty of TLC.

···> *And how does it all translate to an "average day at the office" at Faile?*

Slicing and dicing . . . printing and painting . . . On some days, it is like being a ringmaster in a circus, depending on the how ambitious the upcoming show is!

Faile ∾

STAR SPANGLED SHADOWS · 2009 · ART PRINT *(top)*
CLIENT Personal PRINTER Self-printed PRINTING Screen-print

Faile ⌁

SEX ADS · 2009 · POSTER *(top left)*
WHEN LEGENDS DREAM · 2009 · POSTER *(right)*
CLIENT Personal PRINTER Self-printed PRINTING Screen-print

TENDER FOREVER · 2009 · ART PRINT *(bottom left)*
CLIENT Personal PRINTER Self-printed PRINTING Letterpress
25-color print!

Faile ↝

SHANGHAI BUNNY BOY · 2009 · ART PRINT *(top)*
SINFUL PLEASURES · 2009 · ART PRINT *(left)*
MY CONFESSIONS · 2009 · ART PRINT *(bottom)*
CLIENT Personal PRINTER Self-printed PRINTING Screen-print

Hero Design ✴

BLACK REBEL MOTORCYCLE CLUB · ST. LOUIS · 2008 · POSTER *(left page)*
CLIENT Black Rebel Motorcycle Club PRINTER Self-printed PRINTING Screen-print · Hand-built vacuum table press

DETROIT COBRAS · 2007 · POSTER *(bottom left)*
CLIENT Detroit Cobras PRINTER Self-printed PRINTING Screen-print · Hand-built vacuum table press

Modern Dog Design ✴

THE VENTURES · 2009 · POSTER *(top right)*
CLIENT Seattle Theatre Group PRINTER D + L PRINTING Screen-print
The red screen was made by hand cutting rubylith with an x-acto blade. I liked the original red color of the material, so I carried that through in the ink color. The type was hand-drawn in pencil before being inked with a trusty Micron pen.
DESIGNER *Robert Zwiebel*

BLITZEN TRAPPER · 2009 · POSTER *(bottom right)*
CLIENT Chop Suey PRINTER D + L PRINTING Screen-print
Blitzen Trapper's song "Furr" (about a wolf pack) was the inspiration behind this piece. The wolf was created from a wood-block print and the type was hand-drawn drool.
DESIGNER *Robert Zwiebel*

Soulseven ✴

SQUAD 19 PROMO · 2007 · POSTER *(bottom middle)*
CLIENT Squad 19 PRINTER Squad 19 PRINTING Screen-print
DESIGNER *Sam Soulek* CREATIVE DIRECTOR *Steve Tenebrini* AGENCY *Soulseven*

Hero Design ✍

TEST PRINT, ONE-OF-A-KIND MONO · 2009 · ART PRINT POSTER *(top left, bottom)*
CLIENT Personal PRINTER Self-printed PRINTING Screen-print · Hand-built vacuum table press

I HEART MY BIKE · 2009 · POSTER *(top middle)*
CLIENT Personal PRINTER Self-printed PRINTING Screen-print · American Tempo

MAGNOLIA ELECTRIC COMPANY · 2009 · POSTER *(top right)*
CLIENT Magnolia Electric Company PRINTER Self-printed PRINTING Screen-print · American Tempo

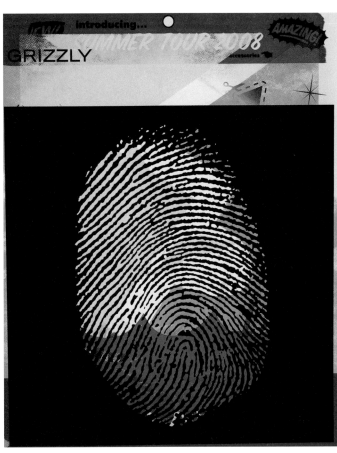

Hero Design ⌁

TEST PRINT, ONE-OF-A-KIND MONO · 2009 · ART PRINT POSTER *(3 images)*
CLIENT Personal PRINTER Self-printed PRINTING Screen-print - Hand-built vacuum table press

SHE AND HIM TOUR · 2008 · POSTER *(bottom)*
CLIENT Zeitgeist Artist Management, LTD PRINTER Self-printed PRINTING Screen-print - American
Tempo

Hero Design ⌁

TRAGICALLY HIP LIVE AT ARTPARK · 2009 · POSTER *(left page)*
CLIENT Funtimes Presents PRINTER Self-printed PRINTING Screen-print - American Tempo

GIRL TALK · 2007 · POSTER *(top right)*
CLIENT Girl Talk PRINTER Self-printed PRINTING Screen-print - Hand-built vacuum table press

MATISYAHU SAN FRANCISCO · 2008 · POSTER *(bottom right)*
CLIENT T.A.O. Management PRINTER Self-printed PRINTING Screen-print - Hand-built vacuum table press

Todd Slater ⌁

THE KILLERS · 2004 · POSTER *(top left)*
CLIENT Patrick McNamara PRINTER D&L PRINTING Screen-print

Inky Lips Press ⌁

VEGAS VIC - SELF-PROMOTION · 2009 · POSTER *(bottom left)*
CLIENT Personal PRINTER Inky Lips Press PRINTING Letterpress - Vandercook Universal lll
Hand-carved linoleum and wood type.
DESIGNER *Casey McGarr*

Märt Infanger | Ultrabazar ↝

ULTRABAZAR · 2003 · POSTER *(top left)*
CLIENT Raum 62 PRINTER Bösch Siebdruck, Stans CH PRINTING Screen-print

ELECTRIC BAZAR CIE · 2008 · CD PACKAGING *(top right)*
CLIENT Electric Bazar Cie PRINTER Printomania, Paris F PRINTING Screen-print

THE WATZLOVES · 2002 · POSTER *(bottom left)*
CLIENT Memphisto Produktion PRINTER Master Rudolph, Lucerne - CH PRINTING Screen-print

Hero Design Studio ↝

TEST PRINT, ONE-OF-A-KIND MONO · 2009 · ART PRINT POSTER *(right page)*
CLIENT Personal PRINTER Self-printed PRINTING Screen-print - Hand-built vacuum table press

MITTWOCH - 19. SEPTEMBER 2007 BOA LUZERN
King KHAN
GREASY-SOUL-FOOD
XXXVI
& THE
SHRINES
(MONTREAL, D)
THE CHIT CHATS
(LUZERN)
DJ WICKED WIGGLER
3048
EINE MEMPHISTO Produktion:
GRAFISTA
Ultra Bazar

Märt Infanger | Ultrabazar ✕

KING KHAN & THE SHRINES · 2008 · POSTER *(left page)*
CLIENT Memphisto Produktion PRINTER Self-printed PRINTING Screen-print

THE CARBONAS · 2008 · POSTER *(left, 2 images)*
CLIENT Memphisto Produktion PRINTER Self-printed PRINTING Screen-print

THE FEELING OF LOVE · 2009 · POSTER *(top right)*
CLIENT Memphisto Produktion PRINTER Self-printed PRINTING Screen-print

Methane ๛

NEKO CASE BIRD · 2009 · POSTER *(top left)*
CLIENT Ok Productions PRINTER Ingram Screen PRINTING Screen-print

SONIC YOUTH · 2009 · POSTER *(top right)*
CLIENT Sonic Youth PRINTER Methane Studios, Inc. PRINTING Screen-print

DINOSAUR JR · 2009 · POSTER *(bottom left)*
CLIENT Dinosaur Jr PRINTER Ingram Screen PRINTING Screen-print

MOGWAI · 2009 · POSTER *(bottom right)*
CLIENT Mogwai PRINTER Ingram Screen PRINTING Screen-print

The Heads of State ๛

TALVIN SINGH · 2006 · POSTER *(right page)*
CLIENT Starbucks PRINTER D&L PRINTING Screen-print

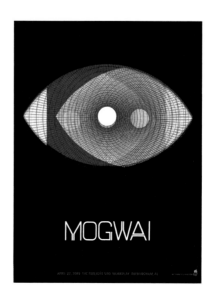

CURATED BY
DJ SPOOKY
THAT SUBLIMINAL KID

TALVIN SINGH & ASHA PUTHLI WITH SPECIAL GUESTS DEWEY REDMAN • GURU • SOLAR & DJ DOO WOP • PREFUSE 73 • OUTERNATIONAL
SUNDAY, AUGUST 13, 2006, GATES OPEN AT 1:30PM **CENTRAL PARK SUMMERSTAGE**

The Little Friends of Printmaking ↝

ANDREW BIRD · 2009 · POSTER *(top left)*
CLIENT Andrew Bird PRINTER Self-printed PRINTING Screen-print
Three-color print.

VISIT CHICAGO · 2008 · ART PRINT *(top right)*
CLIENT   PRINTER Self-printed PRINTING Screen-print
One-color metallic black-ink print.

SONIC YOUTH · 2009 · POSTER *(bottom left)*
CLIENT Sonic Youth PRINTER Self-printed PRINTING Screen-print
Three-color print.

BEASTS! HUNDRED-HANDED GIANT · 2006 · ART PRINT *(bottom right)*
CLIENT Fantagraphics PRINTER Self-printed PRINTING Screen-print
This image was originally designed as a four-color image for the Fantagraphics release "Beasts!". We
remade it as a seven-color silkscreened art print.

The Little Friends of Printmaking ↵

PACIFIC JAMZZZ · 2007 · ART PRINT *(top)*
CLIENT Tiny Showcase PRINTER Self-printed PRINTING Screen-print
Four-color print.

THE INSIDE TRIP · 2008 · ART PRINT *(middle left)*
CLIENT Tiny Showcase PRINTER Self-printed PRINTING Screen-print
Four-color print.

WEENIE · 2009 · ART PRINT *(bottom left)*
CLIENT Personal PRINTER Self-printed PRINTING Screen-print
Three-color print.

YEAR OF THE OX · 2009 · ART PRINT *(bottom right)*
CLIENT Personal PRINTER Self-printed PRINTING Screen-print
Four-color print.

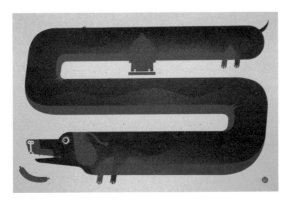

dark meat
with Bunnygrunt

the felice brothers
with AA Bondy

SEPT.25 **DARKER MY LOVE**

DAMIEN JURADO SEPT.26
with Miles Benjamin Anthony Robinson
and Theodore

SEPT.30 AWESOME COLOR

Billiken Club   All ages   8pm   Free

OCT. 25th - PARTS AND LABOR
with SPECIAL GUEST and THE NATURAL SELECTION

BILLIKEN CLUB
Gentleman Auction House
NOV. 15 Bound Stems and Yea Big & Kid Static
★ DOORS 8PM ★ ALL AGES ★ FREE! ★
SLU Campus · 20 N.Grand · STLMO 63103

BILLIKEN CLUB
NOV. 19 **REPUBLIC TIGERS**
with MALPAIS

NOV. 21 **MARNIE STERN**

DEC. 05 **DAVID BAZAN**
and VIA AUDIO

Doors
8PM
All ages
FREE!
SLU CAMPUS
20 N GRAND
STLMO 63103

January 27
**SOMEONE STILL
LOVES YOU
BORIS YELTSIN**
with Pico vs the Island
and Light Pollution
January 31
MAHJONGG
with Emperor X

BILLIKEN CLUB
DOORS AT 8PM - ALL AGES - FREE!
SLU CAMPUS · 20 N. Grand · St. Louis, MO 63103

March 17th
RA RA RIOT
with MAPS & ATLASES

Mar.30 THE **BOWERBIRDS**
with Scotland Yard Gospel Choir
Mar.31 **SPINTO BAND**
with Rural Alberta Advantage
ACCEPTING DONATIONS TO BENEFIT THE URBAN STUDIO
MORE INFO: WWW.THEURBANSTUDIO.BLOGSPOT.COM
BILLIKEN CLUB - Doors at 8 - All ages - FREE!
SLU CAMPUS   20 N. GRAND   STLMO 63103

BEACH HOUSE
April 3rd - with RAGLANI

so many dynamos

junior boys

william fitzsimmons

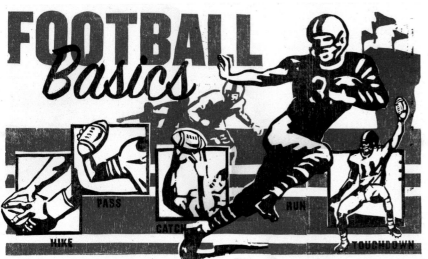

Firecracker Press ᷧ

BILLIKEN CLUB CONCERT SERIES · 2008-2009 · POSTERS *(left page)*
CLIENT Saint Louis University Billiken Club PRINTER Self-printed PRINTING Letterpress - Vandercook SP 20
For the series of concerts during the 2008-2009 school year. All images were hand-carved into wood and the text was hand-set with lead and wood type, then letterpress-printed.

HOW TO DUNK, LEARN TO PITCH LIKE A PRO, FOOTBALL BASICS · 2009 · POSTERS *(this page)*
CLIENT Land of Nod PRINTER Self-printed PRINTING Letterpress - Vandercook SP20
Designed as wall decor for a child's room - children of all ages! Letterpress-printed with hand-carved wood blocks.

september

mon	tue	wed	thu	fri	sat	sun
1	2	3	4	5	6	7
8	9	10	11	12	13	14
15	16	17	18	19	20	21
22	23	24	25	26	27	28
29	30					

www.peopletree.co.uk

november

mon	tue	wed	thu	fri	sat	sun
					1	2
3	4	5	6	7	8	9
10	11	12	13	14	15	16
17	18	19	20	21	22	23
24	25	26	27	28	29	30

www.peopletree.co.uk

Chris Haughton ⌃

PEOPLE TREE · 2008 · CALENDAR *(5 images)*
CLIENT Personal PRINTER Self-printed PRINTING Screen-print
Calendar for people tree fair trade cooperative Bangladesh.

january

mon	tue	wed	thu	fri	sat	sun
1	2	3	4	5	6	
7	8	9	10	11	12	13
14	15	16	17	18	19	20
21	22	23	24	25	26	27
28	29	30	31			

www.peopletree.co.uk

may

mon	tue	wed	thu	fri	sat	sun
			1	2	3	4
5	6	7	8	9	10	11
12	13	14	15	16	17	18
19	20	21	22	23	24	25
26	27	28	29	30	31	

www.peopletree.co.uk

june

mon	tue	wed	thu	fri	sat	sun
						1
2	3	4	5	6	7	8
9	10	11	12	13	14	15
16	17	18	19	20	21	22
23	24	25	26	27	28	29
30					www.peopletree.co.uk	

Firecracker Press ⤴

GRADE A, QUEEN B, VITAMIN C · 2009 · POSTERS *(3 images)*
CLIENT Personal PRINTER Self-printed PRINTING Letterpress - Master Printer Sign Press
Design inspired by everyday language and vintage signage. Hand-carved woodblocks, 1 of 3 in ABC series.

RIVER CITY · 2008 · POSTER *(bottom left)*
CLIENT Personal PRINTER Self-printed PRINTING Letterpress - Vandercook SP 20
Poster design inspired by the City of Saint Louis flag. This symbolizes the confluence of the Missouri and Mississippi rivers. Over the point of confluence lies a round golden disk, upon which is the fleur-de-lis of France, calling attention to the French background of the early city. Printed with hand-carved woodcuts and pressure printing.

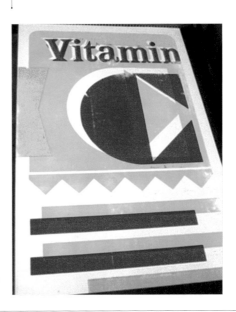

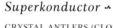

Superkonductor ⌃

CRYSTAL ANTLERS (CLOSE UP) · 2009 · POSTER *(top left)*
CLIENT Empty Bottle Productions PRINTER Self-print PRINTING Screen-print

SKIRT THE GRIDLOCK · 2009 · POSTER *(top right)*
CLIENT Bridgeport WPA PRINTER Self-print PRINTING Screen-print

A/V MURDER · 2008 · POSTER *(middle left)*
CLIENT A/V Murder PRINTER Self-print PRINTING Screen-print

THE MAE SHI (CLOSE UP) · 2009 · POSTER *(middle right)*
CLIENT Post Honeymoon PRINTER Self-print PRINTING Screen-print

THE TYRADES · 2002 · POSTER *(bottom)*
CLIENT Tyrades PRINTER Self-print PRINTING Screen-print

DESIGNER (ALL) *David Head*

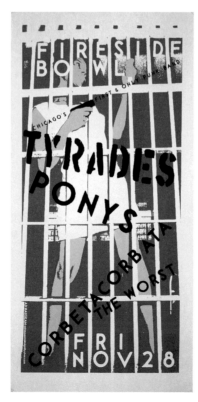

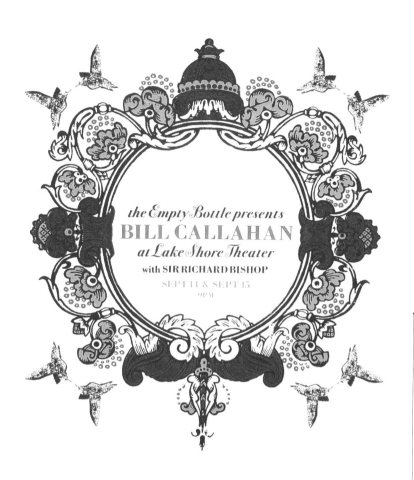

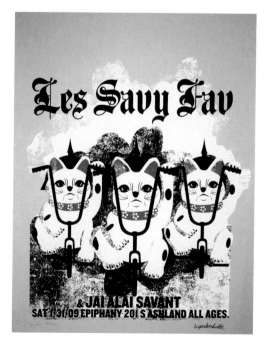

Superkonductor ✌

THE DIALS · 2008 · POSTER *(top left)*
CLIENT The Dials PRINTER Self-print PRINTING Screen-print

BILL CALLAHAN · 2007 · POSTER *(top right)*
CLIENT Empty Bottle Productions PRINTER Self-print PRINTING Screen-print

FIERY FURNACES · 2007 · POSTER *(bottom left)*
CLIENT Empty Bottle Productions PRINTER Self-print PRINTING Screen-print

BLACK LIPS · 2008 · POSTER *(bottom middle)*
CLIENT Empty Bottle Productions PRINTER Self-print PRINTING Screen-print

LES SAVY FAV · 2009 · POSTER *(bottom right)*
CLIENT Empty Bottle Produuctions PRINTER Self-print PRINTING Screen-print

DESIGNER (ALL) *David Head*

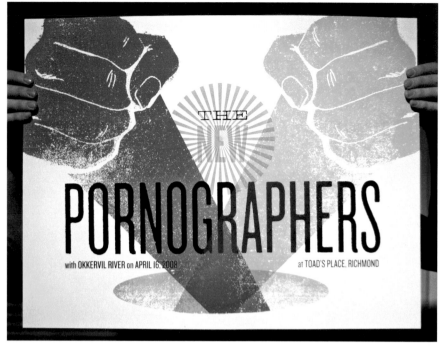

Public Domain ✦

NEW PORNOGRAPHERS POSTER · 2008 · POSTER *(top, bottom left)*
CLIENT Toad's Place, Richmond, VA   PRINTER Self-printed   PRINTING Screen-print
Three-color screen-print poster.

WORK TOGETHER POSTER · 2009 · POSTER *(bottom right)*
CLIENT Personal   PRINTER Self-printed   PRINTING Screen-print
Three-color screen-print poster.

DESIGNER *Matt Pamer*

The Little Friends of Printmaking ⌁

CALL OF THE MYSTIC FROG · 2008 · ART PRINT *(top left)*
CLIENT Personal PRINTER Self-printed PRINTING Screen-print
Three-color silkscreened art print.

END TIMES BOOGALOO · 2008 · ART PRINT *(top right)*
CLIENT Amble Gallery PRINTER Self-printed PRINTING Screen-print
Three-color silkscreened art print.

COSMIC DRAWER · 2008 · ART PRINT *(bottom)*
CLIENT Poketo PRINTER Self-printed PRINTING Screen-print
Three-color silkscreened art print.

WE'VE ★ MOVED

NEW STUDIO and NEW STORE

The FiReCRaCKeR PReSS.

www.firecrackerpress.com

APRIL 10 ✧ INSTITUTE OF CONTEMPORARY ART ✧ BOSTON, MA

Firecracker Press ✍

WE'VE MOVED · 2008 · POSTCARD *(left page)*
CLIENT Personal PRINTER The Firecracker Press PRINTING Letterpress - Vandercook #4
Front of a postcard sent to all of our associates, clients, & friends, announcing our relocation just
down the street from our previous location - "a smooth strut down the lane, yet attention grabbing!"

F2 Design ✍

THE BOOKS · 2009 · POSTER *(top left)*
CLIENT The Books PRINTER f2design PRINTING Letterpress - Proofing press
DESIGNER *Dirk Fowler*

Hero Design Studio ✍

THE LEMONHEADS · 2007 · POSTER *(top right)*
CLIENT Funtimes Presents PRINTER Self-printed PRINTING Screen-print - Hand-built vacuum
table press

DEER · 2008 · POSTER *(bottom left)*
CLIENT Personal PRINTER Self-printed PRINTING Screen-print - Hand-built vacuum table press

The Heads of State ✍

RENE DECARTES · 2009 · EDITORIAL ILLUSTRATION / ART PRINT *(bottom right)*
CLIENT Real Simple PRINTER Half and Half PRINTING Screen-print

REMIND YOURSELF:

I AM A

HUMAN
BEING

BEFORE

ANYTHING
ELSE

LITTLE
IDEAS
BECOME
BIG
BIG
IDEAS
BECOME
LITTLE

Frank Chimero ✦

HUMAN BEING · 2008 · POSTER *(top left)*
BIG IDEAS, LITTLE IDEAS · 2008 · POSTER *(top right)*
DESIGN ENVY · 2008 · POSTER *(bottom left)*
CLIENT Personal PRINTER Self-printed PRINTING Screen-print
Part of an on-going personal project of inspirational posters containing creative maxims and mottos.

The Heads of State ✦

A.C. NEWMAN CONCERT POSTER · 2009 · POSTER *(bottom middle)*
CLIENT A.C. Newman PRINTER Kangaroo Press PRINTING Screen-print

Andrio Abero | 33rpm ✦

DO MAKE SAY THINK · 2007 · POSTER *(bottom right)*
CLIENT New York Society for Ethical Culture PRINTER Lucky Bunny PRINTING Screen-print

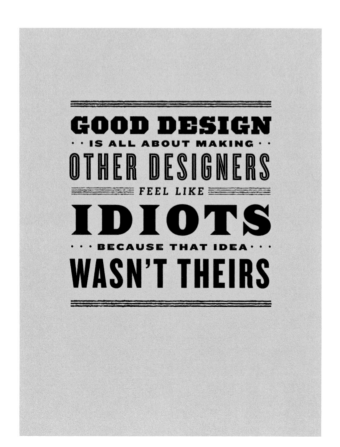

GOOD DESIGN
· · IS ALL ABOUT MAKING · ·
OTHER DESIGNERS
FEEL LIKE
IDIOTS
· · · BECAUSE THAT IDEA · · ·
WASN'T THEIRS

LOVES YOU NO MATTER WHAT YOU LOOK LIKE.

Soulseven

PASTRAMI JACK'S - BEER POSTER · 2009 · POSTER *(top left & bottom right)*
CLIENT Pastrami Jack's PRINTER Self-printed PRINTING Screen-print
This is part of a poster series that was done for Pastrami Jack's, a local deli. Ten posters were produced with each one representing a different offering of the deli.
DESIGNER/ILLUSTRATOR *Sam Soulek* CREATIVE DIRECTOR *Bruce Edwards* COPYWRITER *Sam Soulek*
AGENCY *FAME - A Retail Branding Agency*

Andrio Abero | 33rpm

DAVID BYRNE & BRIAN ENO · 2009 · POSTER *(bottom left)*
CLIENT Live Nation PRINTER D&L Screenprinting PRINTING Screen-print

F2 Design

DEVOTCHKA · 2009 · POSTER *(bottom middle)*
CLIENT Daniel Fluitt PRINTER Self-printed PRINTING Letterpress - Proofing press
DESIGNER *Dirk Fowler*

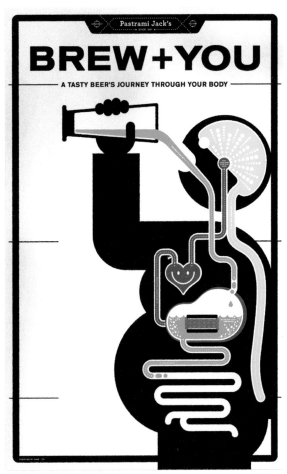

Frank Chimero ᴖ

PRODUCTIVITY · 2008 · POSTER *(top left)*
CLIENT Self-Initiated PRINTER Self-printed PRINTING Screen-print
Part of an on-going personal project of inspirational posters containing creative maxims and mottos.

Hero Design Studio ᴖ

RA RA RIOT · 2009 · POSTER *(bottom left)*
CLIENT Ra Ra Riot PRINTER Hero Design Studio PRINTING Screen-print - American Tempo

Soulseven ᴖ

FAME - ECO FREAKO CAMPAIGN · 2008 · POSTER *(right)*
CLIENT Fame PRINTING Screen-print
DESIGNER/ILLUSTRATOR *Jessica Keintz, Sam Soulek* CREATIVE DIRECTOR *Cheryl Meyer* COPYWRITER *Julie Feyerer* AGENCY *FAME - A Retail Branding Agency*

VELVET LOUNGE ON U STREET
APRIL 12, 2008 • DOORS 9 • SHOW 10
$8 DOLLARS • 21+

Hero Design ᴧ

BETH AND MARK WEDDING · 2007 · POSTER *(top left)*
CLIENT Hero Design Studio PRINTER Self-printed PRINTING Screen-print - Hand-built vacuum table press

DECEMBERISTS · 2007 · POSTER *(bottom right)*
CLIENT Decemberists PRINTER Self-printed PRINTING Screen-print - Hand-built vacuum table press

Frank Chimero ᴧ

CLOSER LEE & THE HEAVY SEAS POSTER · 2008 · POSTER *(top right)*
CLIENT Closer Lee & The Heavy Seas PRINTER Self-printed PRINTING Screen-print

Todd Slater ᴧ

WEEN • 2008 • POSTER *(bottom left)*
CLIENT Ween PRINTER D&L screenprinting PRINTING Screen-print

Methane ↝

DAVE MATTHEWS CINCI HENNA · 2009 · POSTER *(left page)*
CLIENT Dave Matthews Band PRINTER Ingram Screen PRINTING Screen-print

Public Domain ↝

CHARITY:WATER · 2009 · POSTER *(top right)*
CLIENT Charity:Water PRINTER Self-printed PRINTING Screen-print
One-color screen-print poster for Charity:Water

THE DECEMBERISTS · 2009 · POSTER *(bottom, 2 images)*
CLIENT Charlottesville Pavilion PRINTER Self-printed PRINTING Screen-print
Three-color ccreen-print poster on craft paper stock .

DESIGNER (ALL): *Matt Pamer*

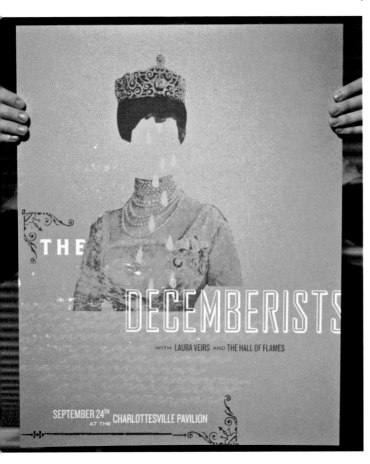

El Jefe ↝

THE RAVEONETTES · DC · 2009 · POSTER *(top)*
CLIENT The Raveonettes PRINTER Grand Palace PRINTING Screen-print

SWEET · 2008 · POSTER *(bottom)*
CLIENT University of Maryland PRINTER Students of UMD PRINTING Screen-print
DESIGNER (ALL) *Jeffrey Everett*

Type B Press ↝

MODEST MOUSE POSTER · 2008 · POSTER *(left)*
CLIENT One Percent Productions PRINTER Self-printed PRINTING Letterpress - 12x18 Chandler & Price
This poster was printed from cut linoleum blocks by Suzanne Holzworth, and wood and metal type.
In each of the blocks is a subtle balloon shape. Modest Mouse has used hot-air balloons a great deal in
their materials. There is also a small balloon debossed into the top-right corner of the poster.
DESIGNER *Bennett Holzworth* ARTWORK *Suzanne Holzworth*

El Jefe ⌁

MY MORNING JACKET - PA · 2008 · POSTER *(top)*
CLIENT My Morning Jacket PRINTER Grand Palace PRINTING Screen-print

RA RA RIOT · 2009 · POSTER *(bottom left)*
CLIENT Ra Ra Riot Club PRINTER Grand Palace PRINTING Screen-print

MY MORNING JACKET - DC · 2008 · POSTER *(bottom right)*
CLIENT My Morning Jacket PRINTER Grand Palace PRINTING Screen-print

DESIGNER (ALL) *Jeffrey Everett*

SPOON
with Black Nasty · April 21, 2009 · Scoot Inn · Austin, TX

A. Micah Smith ↝

SPOON (TAROT) · 2009 · POSTER *(top left)*
CLIENT Spoon PRINTER Vahalla Studios PRINTING Screen-print
Three-color print on 100# white stock.

AC NEWMAN · 2009 · POSTER *(top right)*
CLIENT AC Newman PRINTER Vahalla Studios PRINTING Screen-print
Three-color print on 100# blue stock.

BOYS LIKE GIRLS & BREATHE CAROLINA · 2009 · POSTER *(bottom left)*
CLIENT Myspace Music PRINTER Vahalla Studios PRINTING Screen-print
Three-color print on 100# white stock

NOEL GALLAGHER · 2006 · POSTER *(bottom right)*
CLIENT Myspace Music PRINTER Vahalla Studios PRINTING Screen-print
Three-color print on 100# white stock.

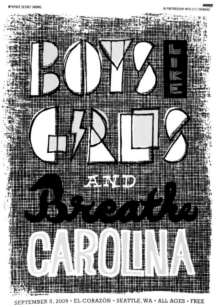

SEPTEMBER 5, 2009 · EL CORAZÓN · SEATTLE, WA · ALL AGES · FREE

A. Micah Smith

FOO FIGHTERS · 2008 · POSTER *(top left)*
CLIENT Eleven Productions PRINTER Vahalla Studios PRINTING Screen-print
Three-color print on 100# white stock.

EXPLOSIONS IN THE SKY · 2008 · POSTER *(top upper right)*
CLIENT Explosions in the Sky PRINTER Vahalla Studios PRINTING Screen-print
Two-color print on 100# natural stock. The two colors over-print to create a third, darker color.

CUTE IS WHAT WE AIM FOR · 2007 · POSTER *(top lower right)*
CLIENT Myspace Music PRINTER Vahalla Studios PRINTING Screen-print
Two-color print on 100# natural stock. Holes drilled through print to emulate an actual shooting range target.

BATTLES · 2008 · POSTER *(bottom)*
CLIENT Battles PRINTER Vahalla Studios PRINTING Screen-print
Under the motto "Technology & Strategy – GESCO Backstage" and with the help of actual work materials the character of a workbook is created, which authentically visualizes the company's operating methods. This quality is enhanced by the use of a ring binder differently perforated papers, and packaging in a metal box. The artistic challenge was also to combine a clearly structured information medium with the interesting look of a genuine workbook.

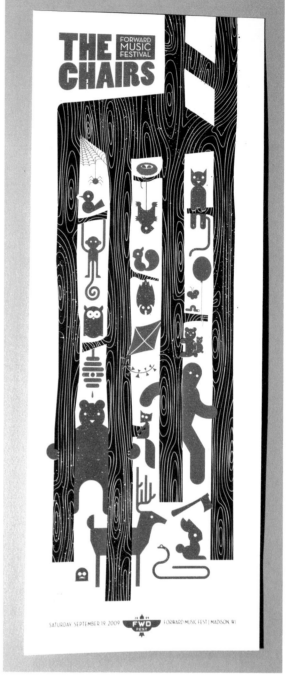

Bandito Design Co. ↶

THE CHAIRS GIG POSTER · 2009 · POSTER *(top left)*
CLIENT Forward Music Festival PRINTER Seizure Palace PRINTING Screen-print
Created for The Chairs.

JOURNALS · 2009 · BOOKLETS *(right)*
CLIENT Personal PRINTER Seizure Palace PRINTING Screen-print

ROLLIN' · 2009 · POSTER *(bottom left)*
CLIENT Personal PRINTER Seizure Palace PRINTING Screen-print

DESIGNER (ALL) *Ryan Brinkerhoff*

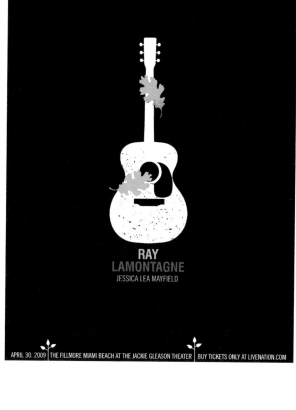

Frank Chimero ↝

ANDREW BIRD POSTER · 2009 · POSTER *(top left)*
CLIENT Forward Music Festival PRINTER Vahalla Studios PRINTING Screen-print

Methane ↝

RAY LAMONTAGEE · 2009 · POSTER *(top right)*
CLIENT Live Nation PRINTER Print Works PRINTING Screen-print
DESIGNER *Robert Lee*

Dotzero Design ↝

48 HOUR FILM PROJECT ,09 POSTER · 2009 · POSTER *(bottom left)*
CLIENT Cinema Syndicate PRINTER Self-printed PRINTING Screen-print
The 48-Hour Film Project gives teams a theme to write, act, film, score and edit a film, all in 48 hours. We designed and printed the poster for the premiere.
DESIGNER *Karen Wippich, Jon Wippich*

Inky Lips Press ↝

COWBOY CAPITAL OF THE WORLD · 2008 · POSTCARD *(bottom right)*
CLIENT Bandera, TX PRINTER Self-printed PRINTING Letterpress - Heidelberg Windmill
DESIGNER *Casey McGarr*

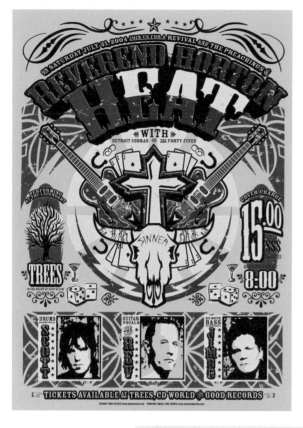

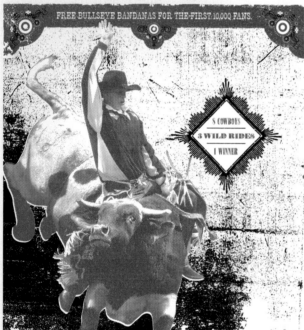

Todd Slater ~

REVEREND HORTON HEAT · 2004 · POSTER *(top left)*
CLIENT The EC PRINTER Diesel Fuel Printing PRINTING Screen-print

OLD 97S · 2004 · POSTER *(top middle)*
CLIENT Dave Mayer PRINTER D&L screenprinting PRINTING Screen-print

DICKEY BETTS · 2004 · POSTER *(top right)*
CLIENT Lee Jobe PRINTER D&L screenprinting PRINTING Screen-print

Soulseven ~

TARGET - WORLD'S TOUGHEST COWBOY · 2007 · NEWSPRINT AD *(bottom)*
CLIENT Target Corporation PRINTING Screen-print
Promotional materials for a traveling rodeo and reality TV show called "World's Toughest Cowboy".
DESIGNER/ILLUSTRATOR *Sam Soulek* CREATIVE DIRECTOR *Bruce Edwards* COPYWRITER *Julie Feyerer*
AGENCY *FAME - A Retail Branding Agency*

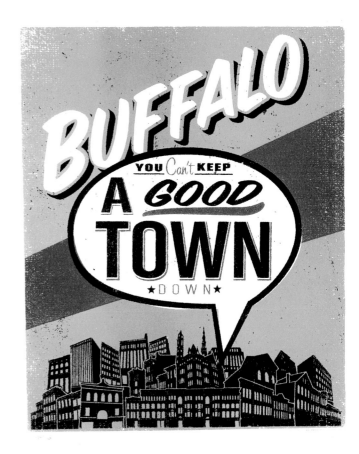

SIAMESE YOUTHS

The Ladies and Gentlemen of Port Perry and its Vicinity are respectfully informed the

SERPENT BROTHERS

MAY BE SEEN AT

The Ink Fountain Circus

ADMISSION ONE SIMOLEON EACH

Hero Design ❧

BUFFALO, STEEL A GREAT CITY · 2009 · POSTER *(top left)*
CLIENT Buffalo Rising PRINTER Self-printed PRINTING Screen-print - American Tempo

CAN'T KEEP A GOOD TOWN DOWN · 2009 · POSTER *(top right)*
CLIENT Buffalo Rising PRINTER Self-printed PRINTING Screen-print - American Tempo

Inky Lips Press ❧

SIAMESE YOUTHS · 2009 · POSTER *(bottom)*
CLIENT Personal PRINTER Inky Lips Letterpress PRINTING Letterpress - Vandercook Universal lll
Hand-carved linoleum, metal and wood type.
DESIGNER *Casey McGarr*

WorkToDate

RECHARGE · 2009 · POSTER *(6 images)*
CLIENT The Art Institute of York Pennsylvania PRINTER Studio On Fire PRINTING Letterpress
Poster to promote their annual alumni exhibit. Limited-edition poster. Printed three spot colors,
letterpressed on French Poptone 65Cover Whip Cream.
DESIGNER *Greg Bennett*

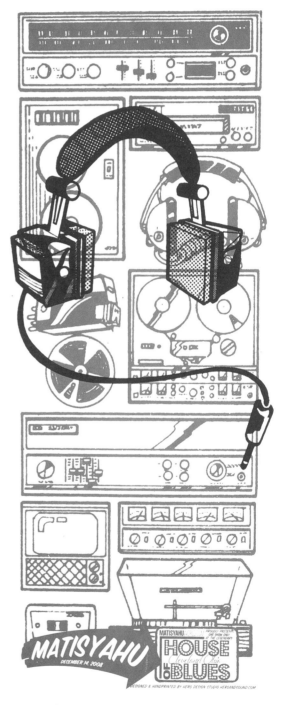

Frank Chimero ↝

BOWERBIRDS TOUR POSTER · 2009 · POSTER *(top left)*
CLIENT Bowerbirds PRINTER Vahalla Studios PRINTING Screen-print

Type B Press ↝

ARTISTS IN RESIDENCE POSTER · 2007 · POSTER *(bottom left)*
CLIENT The Listening Room PRINTER Type B Press PRINTING Letterpress - Vandercook SP15
Artists in Residence is an informal group of local folk-musicians that occasionally perform together. Their diverse make-up was well represented by the random collection of vintage dingbats and random blocks that I had in my letterpress collection.

Hero Design Studio ↝

MATISYAHU CLEVELAND · 2008 · POSTER *(right)*
CLIENT T.A.O. Management PRINTER Self-printed PRINTING Screen-print - Hand-built vacuum table press

The
SWELL SEASON
FEATURING BILL CALLAHAN • SEPTEMBER 20, 2008
AT MASSEY HALL • TORONTO, ONTARIO

THE SO-CAL FIRE POSTER PROJECT

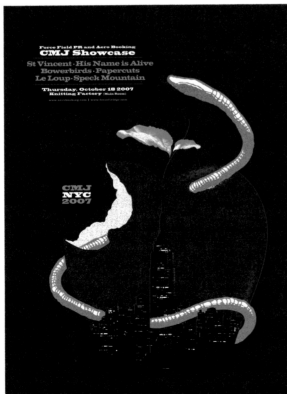

Hero Design ⤴

THE SWELL SEASON · 2008 · POSTER *(left page)*
CLIENT The Swell Season PRINTER Self-printed PRINTING Screen-print · Hand-built vacuum table press

MATISYAHU SAN DIEGO · 2008 · POSTER *(top right)*
CLIENT T.A.O. Management PRINTER Self-printed PRINTING Screen-print · Hand-built vacuum table press

Andrio Abero | 33rpm ⤴

SO-CAL FIRE POSTER PROJECT · 2007 · POSTER *(top left)*
CLIENT So-Cal Fire Poster Project PRINTER D&L Screenprinting PRINTING Screen-print

AERO BOOKING CMJ SHOWCASE · 2007 · POSTER *(bottom)*
CLIENT Aero Booking PRINTER D&L Screenprinting PRINTING Screen-print

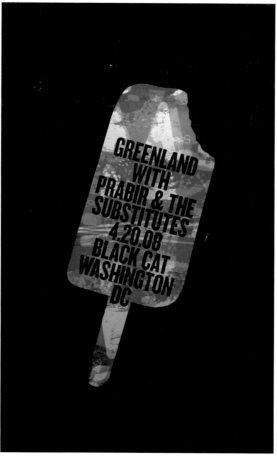

Dirty Pictures ⸙

EXIT CLOV · 2008 · POSTER *(top left)*
CLIENT Exit Clov PRINTER Self-printed PRINTING Screen-print

TWO IF BY SEA · 2006 · POSTER *(top right)*
CLIENT Two if by Sea PRINTER Self-printed PRINTING Screen-print

POPSICLE · 2008 · POSTER *(bottom right)*
CLIENT Greenland PRINTER Self-printed PRINTING Screen-print

DESIGNER (ALL) *Anthony Dihle*

F2 ⸙

AMERICAN ANALOG SET · 2004 · POSTER *(bottom left)*
CLIENT KTXT 88.1 PRINTER Self-printed PRINTING Letterpress - Proofing press
Printed using an actual vinyl LP.

Andrio Abero | 33rpm ☁

VHS OR BETA · 2007 · POSTER *(top left)*
CLIENT Microsoft PRINTER D&L Screenprinting PRINTING Screen-print

COLD WAR KIDS · 2009 · POSTER *(top right)*
CLIENT Live Nation PRINTER D&L Screenprinting PRINTING Screen-print

DOVES · 2009 · POSTER *(bottom left)*
CLIENT Live Nation PRINTER D&L Screenprinting PRINTING Screen-print

BJORK · 2007 · POSTER *(bottom right)*
CLIENT Live Nation PRINTER D&L Screenprinting PRINTING Screen-print
Typography illustration *Justine Ashbee* DESIGNER *Andrio Abero*

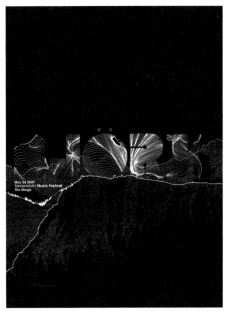

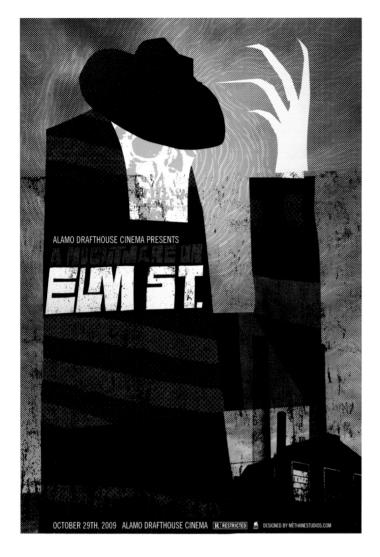

Methane ⋏

ELM STREET · 2008 · POSTER *(top left)*
CLIENT Greg Allman PRINTER Ingram Screenprint PRINTING Screen-print
DESIGNER *Robert Lee*

ROCKING HORSE · 2009 · POSTER *(top right)*
CLIENT Dead Weather PRINTER Ingram Screenprint PRINTING Screen-print
DESIGNER *Robert Lee*

BLITZEN TRAPPER · 2009 · POSTER *(bottom left)*
CLIENT Ok Productions PRINTER Ingram Screenprint PRINTING Screen-print
DESIGNER *Methane studios*

DESIGNER · 2009 · POSTER *(bottom right)*
CLIENT Ok Productions PRINTER Half & Half PRINTING Screen-print
DESIGNER *Robert Lee*

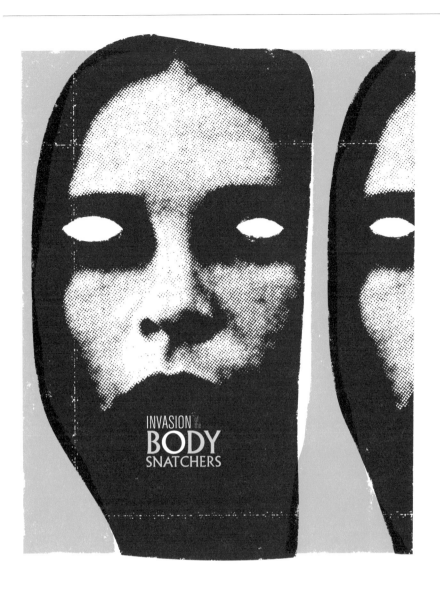

INVASION of the
BODY
SNATCHERS

TERROR THURSDAY PRESENTS Invasion of the Bodysnatchers FREE • NOVEMBER 20TH, 2008
ALAMO DRAFTHOUSE CINEMA AT THE RITZ • 1120 S. LAMAR BLVD • AUSTIN TX 78701 INFO AT WWW.ORIGINALALAMO.COM • POSTER BY THE HEADS OF STATE

Hero Design ↝

BUFFALO SMALL PRESS BOOK FAIR · 2008 · POSTER *(top left)*
CLIENT Buffalo Small Press Book Fair PRINTER Self-printed PRINTING Screen-print - Hand-built
vacuum table press

BUFFALO RISING · 2009 · POSTER *(top right)*
CLIENT Buffalo Rising PRINTER Self-printed PRINTING Screen-print - Hand-built vacuum table press

SPOON · 2007 · POSTER *(bottom left)*
CLIENT Constant Artists Inc. PRINTER Self-printed PRINTING Screen-print - Hand-built vacuum
table press

The Heads of State ↝

INVASION OF THE BODY SNATCHERS · 2008 · POSTER *(bottom right)*
CLIENT Rolling Roadshow PRINTER D&L PRINTING Screen-print

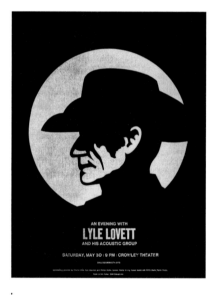

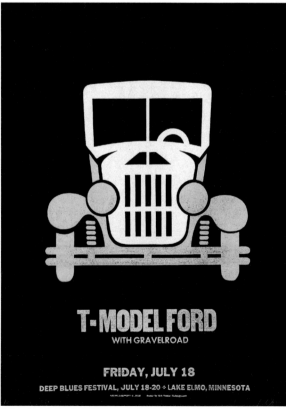

F2 Design ⌐

THE BOOKS NY · 2009 · POSTER *(top left)*
CLIENT The Books PRINTER Self-printed PRINTING Letterpress - Proofing press

WILCO-BOOTS · 2009 · POSTER *(upper top right)*
CLIENT Wilco PRINTER Self-printed PRINTING Letterpress - Proofing press

WILCO-SNEAKERS · 2009 · POSTER *(lower top right)*
CLIENT Wilco PRINTER Self-printed PRINTING Letterpress - Proofing press

LYLE LOVETT · 2009 · POSTER *(middle right)*
CLIENT Ballroom Marfa PRINTER Self-printed PRINTING Letterpress - Proofing press

T-MODEL FORD · 2008 · POSTER *(bottom left)*
CLIENT Deep Blues Festival PRINTER Self-printed PRINTING Letterpress - Proofing press

DESIGNER *Dirk Fowler*

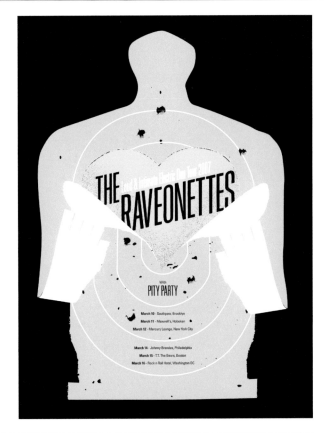

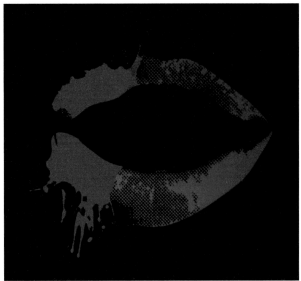

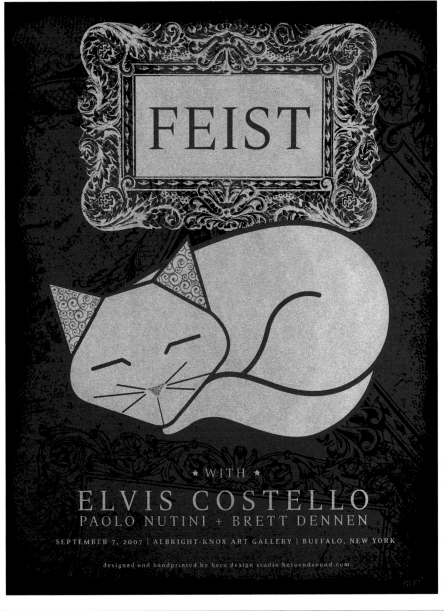

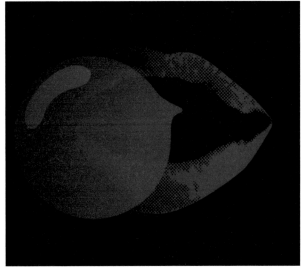

Andrio Abero | 33rpm ᴥ

THE RAVOENETTES · 2007 · POSTER *(top left)*
CLIENT The Raveonettes PRINTER D&L Screenprinting PRINTING Screen-print

Us & Them ᴥ

YUBBLEYUM (PART 1 + 2) · 2009 · ART PRINT *(top right, 2 images)*
CLIENT Personal PRINTER Us & Them PRINTING Serigraphie
A diptych silk-screen, an edition of 50.
DESIGNER *Sei Rey Ho*

Hero Design Studio ᴥ

FEIST · 2007 · POSTER *(bottom)*
CLIENT Albright Knox Art Gallery PRINTER Self-printed PRINTING Screen-print - Hand-built vacuum table press

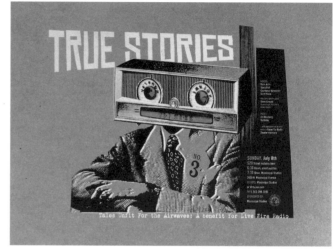

Dotzero Design ·

TRUE STORIES 2, 3, 5, 6 · 2007/8 · POSTERS *(this page)*
TRUE STORIES 4 POSTER · 2007 · POSTER *(right page)*
CLIENT True Stories PRINTER Self-printed PRINTING Screen-print
True Stories is a reading and music performance series that specializes in humor and self-humiliation.
Storytellers and songwriters are featured telling and singing (mostly) true stories.

DESIGNER *Karen Wippich, Jon Wippich*

Dotzero Design ↝

DOTZERO PROMO · 2003 · COASTERS *(top)*
CLIENT Personal PRINTER Pinball Publishing PRINTING Offset
The two of us each designed two coasters. We designed the wrappers shown at the top, but they were printed regular offset.

OPENING INVITATION · 2007 · COASTERS *(middle)*
CLIENT Davis Agency PRINTER Self-printed PRINTING Screen-print
A residential property client of Davis Agency was having a grand opening and they thought mailing out invitations in the form of coasters was a great way to reinforce the idea that it was going to be a fun event with drinks and appetizers.

HOLIDAY · 2006 · COASTERS *(bottom)*
CLIENT Davis Agency PRINTER Self-printed PRINTING Screen-print

DESIGNER (ALL) *Karen Wippich, Jon Wippich*

Dotzero Design ↝

ODDITY CARDS, PACK 1 + 2 · 2007 · GREETING CARDS
CLIENT Personal PRINTER Self-printed PRINTING Screen-print
We designed 8 cards and two bags, printed them and then packaged them in groups of four cards within each bag.

SAD SACKS AND CATS CD · 2008 · CD PACKAGING
CLIENT Summer of Music PRINTER Self-printed PRINTING Screen-print
We each designed two panels of the four panel case. the CDs themselves were printed conventionally.
DESIGNER (ALL) *Jon Wippich, Karen Wippich*

it did not
happen everyday when the citrene
sparkling in the morning sun dissipated into breath.

Blackbird Letterpress ↶

HOLINESS HAYDEN · 2009 · CARDS *(top left & bottom right)*
CLIENT Personal PRINTER Self-printed PRINTING Letterpress - Chandler & Price 8x12
Two-color reduction linoleum cut, hand-set type. This is a pair of cards from a print exchange deck/
project where 32 printers created their own Old Maid cards.

BREATHLESS · 2009 · ART PRINT *(top right)*
CLIENT Personal PRINTER Self-printed PRINTING Letterpress - Vandercook sp20
Two-color multiple linoleum block letterpress printed, hand-set type, hand-cut paper

REVOLUTION · 2007 · ART PRINT *(bottom left)*
CLIENT Personal PRINTER Self-printed PRINTING Woodcut, Serigraphie
Three-color reduction woodcut, One-color serigraph

DESIGNER (ALL): *Kathryn Hunter*

Mark Phelan | Bumper Crop Press ∿

THE GIANT PTERODACTYL OF BIRD HILL · 2009 · POSTER *(top left)*
CLIENT Personal PRINTER Bumper Crop Press PRINTING Letterpress - 1895 Poco Proofing Press
One-color linocut print. Based on legends of the Bridgewater Triangle, a 200 square-miles area in
south eastern Massachusetts where I live, these posters celebrate the supposed paranormal activity
that has haunted this space since colonial times.

CT60 · 2009 · POSTER *(bottom left)*
ORANGE '58 · 2008 · POSTER *(bottom right)*
CLIENT Personal PRINTER Bumper Crop Press PRINTING Letterpress - 1895 Poco Proofing Press
Two-color linocut on paper. These posters harken back to the early days of hotrodding, and celebrate
the excitement of racing and spectating at these drag races.

Elshopo ↝

ANAB & CHIENPO AT JTM GALLERY · 2008 · PANCAKE *(top left)*
CLIENT Personal PRINTER Self-printed PRINTING Elshopo silk-screen machine
Chocolate on pancake. Performance at JTM gallery, Paris. Pancake, T-shirts and postcards produced...

CHE PANCAKE · 2005 · PANCAKE *(top right)*
CLIENT Personal PRINTER Self-printed PRINTING Screen-print - Elshopo printfood machine
Print realised during an anti-capitalist manifestation in Grenoble (FR).

MICHAEL JACKSON BLACK TO WHITE · 2009 · PANCAKE *(upper & lower middle left))*
CLIENT Veduta Biennale de Lyon (FR) PRINTER Self-printed PRINTING Screen-print - Elshopo
silkscreen machine
Printing performance in Lyon the July 5, 2009 in memory of Michael Jackson.

LOUIS SHOPO · 2008 · PANCAKE *(bottom)*
CLIENT Personal PRINTER Self-printed PRINTING Screen-print - Elshopo printfood machine
Printed in Tokyo in 2008.

Elshopo ⌁

PRINTFOOD POSTER · 2009 · POSTER *(4 images)*
CLIENT Personal PRINTER Elshopo PRINTING Screen-print
Poster printed with chocolate yoghurt. edition of 50.

Dotzero Design ᴧ

AUDGEPODGE BUSINESS CARDS · 2008 · BUSINESS CARDS *(top left)*
CLIENT Audge Podge Designs PRINTER Self-printed PRINTING Screen-print
The client hand-makes bags, purses and other items in a vintage style, and wanted a vintage look for her cards. We went to thrift shops and bought stacks of old picture postcards. We printed three business cards per postcard, then trimmed them out. The white ink had to be printed with two hits to cover well enough for the copy to read, but we didn't want it too opaque. We wanted faint images from the postcards to show through. The backs of the cards had old written messages, postmarks and stamps that also showed through some after we printed. No two cards are alike.
DESIGNER *Karen Wippich, Jon Wippich*

RENDON-TANNER WEDDING · 2009 · INVITATION, PROGRAM, RSVP, THANK YOU CARDS, ETC. *(top right)*
CLIENT Rendon-Tanner PRINTER Self-printed PRINTING Screen-print
We usually silkscreen posters and promos, but for a friend we designed and printed all the print pieces for her wedding. We used three colors and printed many things together to cut down on the number of print runs needed.
DESIGNER *Karen Wippich, Jon Wippich*

Funnel: Eric Kass ᴧ

GREEN GENES · 2008 · BRANDING *(bottom)*
CLIENT Green Genes PRINTER Faulkenberg Printing PRINTING Screen-print
Green Genes is an eco-friendly boutique for children and their grown-ups.

BirdDog Press ∾

ENVELOPE BOOK · 2008 · HANDBOUND BOOK *(top left)*
CLIENT Newcomer Family PRINTER BirdDog Press PRINTING Letterpress - Chandler & Price 8x12 NS
Heirloom-quality handbound envelope book with antique wood-type letters and vintage animal illustrations. Letterpress signatures of archival paper, coptic-stitched and interleaved with envelopes for keepsakes. Space for photos, stories, artwork, and more.
DESIGNER *Allison Bozeman*

WOODTYPE BABY ANNOUNCEMENT · 2008 · ANNOUNCEMENT *(top right & bottom left)*
CLIENT Newcomer Family PRINTER BirdDog Press PRINTING Letterpress - Chandler & Price 8x12 NS
Baby Announcement printed with antique wood type and vintage animal illustrations. Matching handbound baby album for Henry & Newcomer Family.
DESIGNER *Allison Bozeman*

Firecracker Press ∾

SASQUATCH HUNT · 2007 · DRINK COASTERS *(top right)*
CLIENT Personal PRINTER The Firecracker Press PRINTING Letterpress - Vandercook #4, die-cut - Chandler & Price
Set of four drink coasters, letterpress printed. Designed as a short story depicted by you: Is it a love affair or a plot to murder?

DEEP SEA · 2009 · GREETING CARDS *(bottom right)*
CLIENT Personal PRINTER The Firecracker Press PRINTING Letterpress - Vandercook #4
Set of four blank cards illustrating beautiful creatures of the sea.

Dotzero Design ✴

US ELECTION POSTER · 2008 · POSTER *(left page)*
CLIENT Moveon.org PRINTER Self-printed PRINTING Screen-print
This was a limited-run piece printed on wood panel. The background was painted with blue latex paint. Then it was silkscreened in white and red. The poster was selected to be auctioned off online with part of the proceeds going to the cause of my choice.

PROMO HEAD/ TYPE HEAD/CLOWN/PAPER ROLL · 2008 · POSTERS *(this page)*
CLIENT Personal PRINTER Self-printed PRINTING Screen-print
We printed four different designs as a promo. We let clients and friends pick which they wanted. They are on wood panel. Each was first roughly hand painted with cream-colored latex paint allowing some of the board's color to show through. Then we silkscreened each in three colors.

DESIGNER (ALL) *Karen Wippich, Jon Wippich*

Jens Bonnke ‑

IF THE DEVIL IS 6 · 2008 · POSTER *(top left)*
CLIENT Personal PRINTER Self-printed Digital print

DOG HEAVEN · 2005 · POSTER *(top right)*
CLIENT Personal PRINTER Self-printed PRINTING Screen-printed

EVACUATE EVERYONE! · 2006 · POSTER *(bottom left)*
CLIENT Personal PRINTER Self-printed PRINTING Digital print

UNTITLED · 2006 · POSTER *(bottom right)*
CLIENT Personal PRINTER Self-printed PRINTING Screen-printed

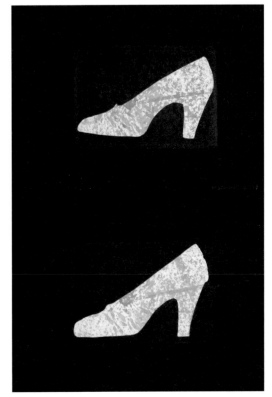

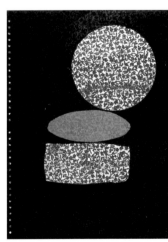

Maki Shimizu ⤳

MEINE KLEINE BLECHBÜCHSE · 2005 · MONOTYPE *(top left)*
CLIENT 44flavours PRINTER Self-printed PRINTING Alugrafie / Papercut printing
44flavours magazine no.02, 2006

HAHN ODER HUHN · 2005 · MONOTYPE *(top right)*
CLIENT Peperoni Books PRINTER Self-printed PRINTING Alugrafie / Papercut printing
"Makis Haustierbuch," Peperoni Books, Berlin 2006

MEINE SCHUHE · 2001 · MONOTYPE *(bottom)*
CLIENT Personal PRINTER Self-printed PRINTING Alugrafie / Papercut printing

Julie Peach ♪

BIRDS & CO. · 2009 · POSTER *(top left & lower right)*
CLIENT Personal PRINTER Self-printed PRINTING Linocut

BIRDS & CO. · 2009 · NAPKINS *(top right)*
CLIENT Personal PRINTER Self-printed PRINTING Linocut on cotton

HELLO NARWHAL· 2008 · ART PRINT *(left)*
CLIENT Personal PRINTER Self-printed PRINTING Linocut

EVERYBODY'S TALKIN · 2008 · NOTEBOOK *(bottom)*
CLIENT Personal PRINTER Self-printed PRINTING Linocut

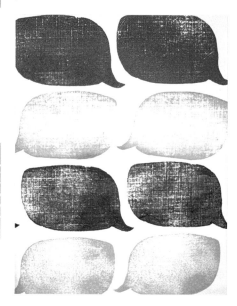

Cristóbal Schmal ⌁

SAO PAULO · 2009 · CARD *(top left)*
CLIENT Collective Project PRINTING None - illustration

WINE · 2009 · COVER *(top right)*
CLIENT Personal PRINTING None - illustration

SINN DES LEBENS · 2008 · CARD *(bottom left)*
CLIENT Personal PRINTING None - illustration

LUNAR PROJECT · 2007 · CARD *(bottom right)*
CLIENT Lunar Project jazz band PRINTING None - illustration

Nobrow •⁄•

Don't give up your day job? In 2008, East London idealists Sam Arthur and Alex Spiro took a huge leap of faith when they decided to swap their careers in short films, animation, and illustration for the rather more precarious existence of publishers and printmakers extraordinaires. United in their unbridled love of printed ephemera and great illustration, they teamed up to form Nobrow, a platform and screen-print workshop that picks exceptional talents from the realm of illustration, and commercial and pervasive art for their in-house magazine and handmade limited-edition book runs. With only 50 to 100 issues printed in Nobrow's own basement, their Small Press Editions are objects to be coveted, collected, and cherished—and often infused with a healthy dash of the surreal. Their themed biannual Nobrow magazine, on the other hand, delves deep into the unknown to return with rich pickings from the far side of contemporary illustration, featuring seasoned veterans like Blexbolex and Pietari Posti, as well as emerging talents eager to spread their creative wings. Limited to 3,000 issues and two colors, issue #1 was printed by one of the few remaining radical print co-operatives from the late 1970s.

···> *What was your initial spark and inspiration for launching Nobrow?*
We are and have always been inspired by the level of attention given to printing processes before the digital age. Don't get me wrong: we're not Luddites and we don't have any problem with technology. We simply don't want to be slaves to what is easiest or most efficient. With this in mind, we try to incorporate analogue processes into the digital framework of our world as much as possible and that is one of the reasons why we often print with spot colors rather than using the traditional CMYK process.

···> *What is the particular allure of screen-printing?*
The tactile nature of it, the way the ink is slightly raised off the paper, the vitality of the colors, the beautiful mistakes that simply cannot be replicated with any process of mass production.

···> *You also do some of your own printing, don't you? Could you take us through the set-up and process?*
The first and most important stages are to do with the preparation of the artwork. If the work is created with screen-printing in mind, the results are usually much more pleasing. Once we have the artwork in place, we work together with the artist to create the right color separations. This process can take quite a lot of time as each project is different and requires a different approach. For example, a certain color overlap can make registration easier, while layering colors on top of each other can have a different outcome whether the inks are transparent or opaque. In addition, different ink colors and brands offer different coverage, so there are many aspects to consider. As there is plenty of experimentation involved, be prepared for a few disappointments when you first start out. There are no short-cuts – be patient and meticulous and eventually you will get the hang of it!

The next step involves creating "positive films" from the color separations used to expose the screens. Put simply, we need a pattern that can be transferred to the screen using a photographic process. To this end, we use either photocopies on thin paper or films created by a linotype image setter. The screens and positives are then exposed to UV light in order to transfer the desired image. Afterwards, they go through a careful washing and drying process before they are ready to use for printing.

We print one color at a time and usually work on editions of 100 or less. Once a color is printed, it is left in the drying rack until the next color is ready to print, and then the process starts all over again. An edition of 50 with four colours can easily take a week from start to finish!

···> *With this elaborate process in mind,—what is the first thing you look for in a new publication? What usually decides if it is worthy of your attention?*
The beauty of the object as a whole, and the quality of the content and the message. We give equal importance to the aesthetic and the conceptual.

···> *Let's move on to the content – your* Nobrow *magazines always focus on a specific theme* (The Jungle, Gods and Monsters) . . .
It is great fun to choose these themes—we always try to pick a subject that would be fun for the artists involved. After all, *Nobrow* is a contribution-based magazine. As the contributing artists do not receive payment for their work, they should at least enjoy it!

···> *What are your selection criteria and parameters for submissions?*
We scour the internet, we look at the printed world that surrounds us—we look for people that have something different to offer in their work and would suit a specific issue.
As *Nobrow* is supposed to be a one-off collectible item, we try to commission exclusive pieces—it would defeat the purpose of the magazine if we featured a lot of published works. When we do include works created for other clients, we usually try to change them slightly, e. g. by playing with the color or format of the image itself, to make them unique to that particular issue. The parameters are usually some sort of color scheme, the issue's chosen topic and our magazine format, but the absence of copy and advertising means that there is a lot of room to breathe. Aside from the basics, the chosen artists are free to do as they please.

···> *What is the concept behind* Small Press Books?
For this run of limited-edition booklets, we approach people whose work would suit the screen-printing process and the format of a small book. It is a very good way to produce a book and try out an idea that might not be possible (financially or technically) within the framework of an offset litho project.

···> *Any secret favourites among your latest projects? And why?*
Abecederia—I think the compositions based around letters of the alphabet are genius. Blexbolex is one of the great illustrators of our times. He has a fundamental understanding of every aspect of the craft—composition, color, narrative, and the technical procedures involved in image reproduction. This allows him to have a level of control over the whole process that results in work that is consistent and undeniably beautiful.

Nobrow ⌄

VENDOIN · 2009 · LIMITED EDITION BOOK *(top, 2 images)*
CLIENT Personal PRINTER Nobrow Small Press PRINTING Screen-print
DESIGNER *Joe Crocker for Nobrow Small Press*

THE BENTO BESTIARY · 2009 · LIMITED EDITION BOOK *(bottom)*
CLIENT Personal PRINTER Nobrow Small Press PRINTING Screen-print
DESIGNER *Joe Crocker for Nobrow Small Press*

Nobrow ✧

NOBROW ISSUE 1: GODS AND MONSTERS · 2009 · MAGAZINE *(top left)*
CLIENT Personal PRINTER Calverts PRINTING Offset print
Two spot color.

THE BENTO BESTIARY · 2009 · LIMITED EDITION BOOK *(top right)*
CLIENT Personal PRINTER Nobrow Small Press PRINTING Screen-print
DESIGNER *Ben Newman for Nobrow Small Press*

BENTO BESTIARY · 2009 · LIMITED EDITION BOOK *(bottom right)*
CLIENT Personal PRINTER Nobrow Small Press PRINTING Screen-print
DESIGNER *Ben Newman for Nobrow Small Press*

NOBROW ISSUE 1: GODS AND MONSTERS · 2009 · MAGAZINE *(bottom left)*
CLIENT Personal PRINTER Calverts PRINTING Offset print
Two spot color. Nobrow Issue 1 was art-directed and designed by Sam Arthur and Alex Spiro
DESIGNER *Paul Blow for Nobrow Issue 1*

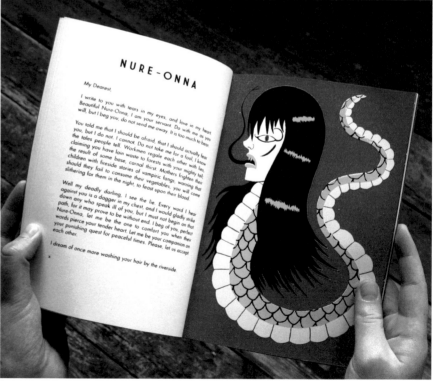

Nobrow ᴧ

ABECEDERIA · 2009 · COMIC BOOK *(top left, lower middle left, bottom left. bottom right))*
CLIENT Personal PRINTER Nobrow Press PRINTING Offset print
Three spot color.
ILLUSTRATOR *Blexbolex* EDITED & PRODUCED *Nobrow: Sam Arthur, Alex Spiro*

NOBROW ISSUE 2: THE JUNGLE · 2009 · MAGAZINE COVER *(top right)*
CLIENT Personal PRINTER Nobrow Press PRINTING Offset print
Three spot color. Cover for Nobrow issue 2 was art directed and edited by Sam Arthur and Alex Spiro.
ILLUSTRATOR *Blexbolex*

NOBROW ISSUE 2: THE JUNGLE · 2009 · MAGAZINE SPREAD *(upper middle left)*
CLIENT Personal PRINTER Nobrow Press PRINTING Offset print
Three spot color. Spread for Nobrow issue 2.
ILLUSTRATOR *Isabelle Vandenabeele*

Alexis Rom Estudio ⌁

MAMBIANDO · 2009 · POSTER *(top left)*
CLIENT Personal PRINTER Self-printed PRINTING Rubber-cut

LAS CORISTAS · 2009 · POSTER *(top right)*
CLIENT Personal PRINTER Self-printed PRINTING Rubber-cut

UNTITLED • 2009 • PHOTOLITHOGRAPHS *(bottom left)*
CLIENT Personal PRINTING None
Selection of handmade photolithograhs for silkscreen printing.

LION GALANT · 2003 · ART PRINT *(bottom right)*
CLIENT Personal PRINTER Self-printed PRINTING Serigraphy
DESIGNER (ALL) *Alexis Rom Estudio ::: Taller Vostok*

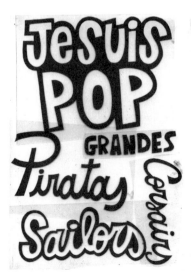

TALLER VOSTOK

Alexis Rom Estudio ↝

JURÁSICA · 2007 · ART PRINT
CLIENT Personal PRINTER Self-printed PRINTING Serigraphy

UNTITLED · 2008 · ART PRINT
CLIENT ChinaTag PRINTER Self-printed PRINTING Serigraphy & stamps
ChinaTag is an italian-chinese furniture brand for which we designed and played a live performance during the Milan Design Week 2008. We printed a series of 250 slightly different prints, combining one-color serigraphy and stamps.

CAFÉ METRO · 2009 · POSTER
CLIENT Personal PRINTER Self-printed PRINTING Rubber-cuts
Rubber-cuts are relief prints made by cutting silicone sheets. A main series of them were exhibited in Mondo Vostok, Galería Garabat, Bilbao (April-June 2009).

DESIGNER *Alexis Rom Estudio ::: Taller Vostok*

Alexis Rom Estudio ⸙

CUT OUT PAPER SHAPES · 2009 · PAPER CUTS *(3 images)*
CLIENT Personal PRINTER None PRINTING Screen-print
Cut-out paper is one of our favorite graphic techniques. We use these shapes directly for preparing photolithographs for silkscreen printing, or we scan them for digital composition.
DESIGNER *Alexis Rom Estudio ::: Taller Vostok* PHOTO *Melina Mulas*

Chris Thornley ⸙

MORE REASONS TO NOT GO CAMPING · 2007 · POSTER *(right page)*
CLIENT Threadless PRINTER Dan Grzeca PRINTING Screen-print

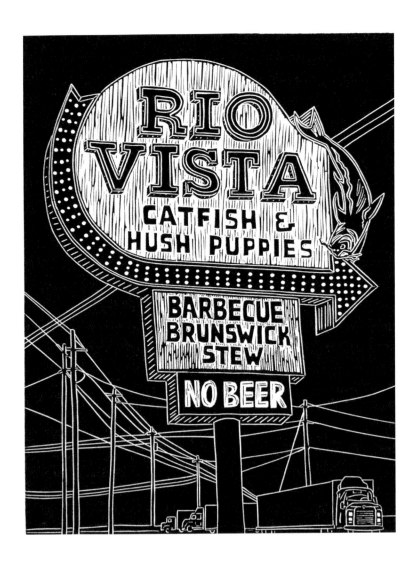

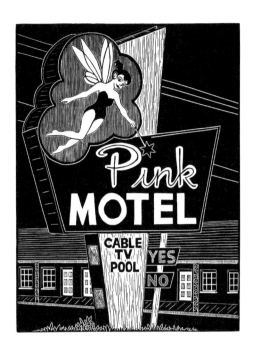

Katherine W. Linn ↝

THE GEORGIAN TERRACE · 2005 · ART PRINT *(left page)*
THE PINK MOTEL · 2008 · ART PRINT *(top left)*
RIO VISTA · 2003 · ART PRINT *(top right)*
PETE'S HOT DOGS · 2007 · ART PRINT *(middle left)*
KRISPY KREME · 2009 · ART PRINT *(bottom left)*
THE BLUEBIRD TRUCK STOP · 2004 · ART PRINT *(bottom right)*
CLIENT Personal PRINTER Self-printed PRINTING Linocut
DESIGNER (ALL) *Katherine W. Linn*

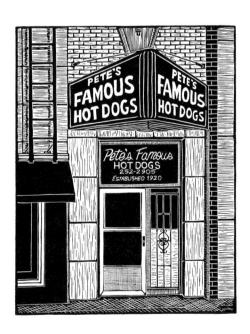

Visual

MAGAZINE DE DISEÑO, CREATIVIDAD
GRAFICA Y COMUNICACIÓN
NÚMERO 139. AÑO XXI. 7.21

Alexis Rom Estudio ⌐

VISUAL, ISSUE 139 · 2009 · MAGAZINE COVER *(left page)*
CLIENT Visual PRINTER None PRINTING Rubber-stamp print

BISH FATFACE STAMPS · 2006 · RUBBER CAST TYPE *(top)*
CLIENT Personal PRINTER None PRINTING Rubber-stamp print

MANKIND EGYPTIAN TYPEFACE · 2006 · PHOTOPOLYMER TYPE *(right)*
CLIENT Personal PRINTER None PRINTING Rubber-stamp print
Photopolymer type, set with rubber band.

EGYPTIAN TYPEFACE (STUDY) · 2006 · CARVED RUBBER STAMPS *(bottom)*
CLIENT Personal PRINTER None PRINTING Rubber-stamp print

DESIGNER (ALL) *Taller Vostok* PHOTOS (ALL) *Melina Mulas*

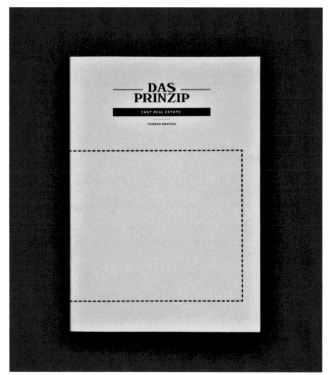

Bordfunk | Matthias Hübner ⤳

DAS PRINZIP ZAST REAL ESTATE · 2009 · BOOK COVER *(6 images)*
CLIENT Städtisches Kunstmuseum Spendhaus Reutlingen PRINTER Self-printed PRINTING
Rubber-stamp print
DESIGNER *Matthias Hübner with Thomas Bratzke*

Documenting the project Zast Real Estate, the book gives an insight in the working process of the artist. Zast Real Estate acts as a temporary real estate office, inviting the people around it to comment and improve places in the neighborhood by offering descriptions and images of these places. For the catalogue cover we decided to treat in a way, as all the particpants of Thomas project did with the proposals, so we had all six symbols from the instrcutions transfered to rubber stamps and made each one of the 500 edition by hand and indivually.

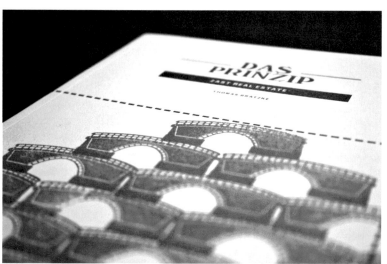

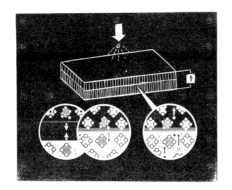

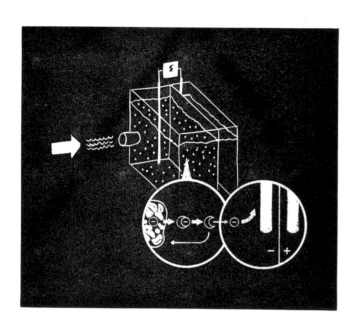

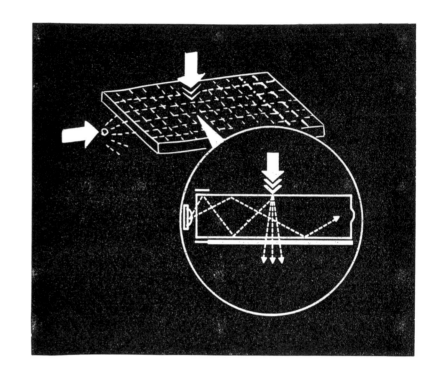

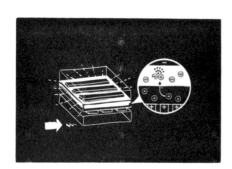

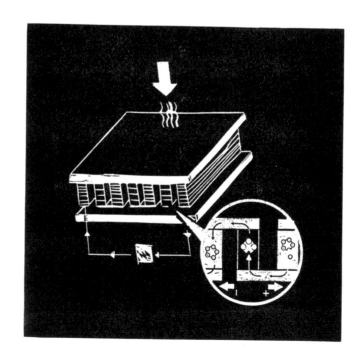

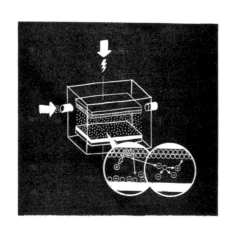

Onlab | Nicolas Bourquin ↝

SMART SURFACES AND THEIR APPLICATION IN ARCHITECTURE AND DESIGN · 2009 · BOOK ILLUSTRATIONS *(both pages, 12 images)*
CLIENT Birkhäuser PRINTER Klaus Regel, Berlin PRINTING Linoprints
Book, 184 pages, 460 illustrations (230 in color). The linocuts were developed and produced (cut by hand and mechanically) for the book project to visualize components, processes, production methods, application of diverse surfaces.
ART DIRECTION *onlab, Nicolas Bourquin, Thibaud Tissot* ILLUSTRATIONS & LINOCUTS *onlab, Nicolas Bourquin, Marte Meling Enoksen, Maike Hamacher, Matthias Hübner* PROJECT COORDINATION *onlab, Judith Wimmer* EDITOR *Thorsten Klooster* AUTHORS *Niels Boing, Simon Davis, Thorsten Klooster, Almut Seeger*

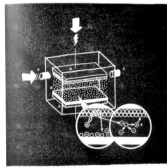

◀ DOWN THE LINE ▶

CALLAHAN

LIVE

www.callahan.ch

Dynamo | Thibaud Tissot & Yassin Baggar ⊹

DOWN THE LINE · 2009 · CD/POSTER/POSTCARD *(3 images)*
CLIENT Callahan PRINTER Self-printed PRINTING Linocut
DESIGNER *Thibaud Tissot*

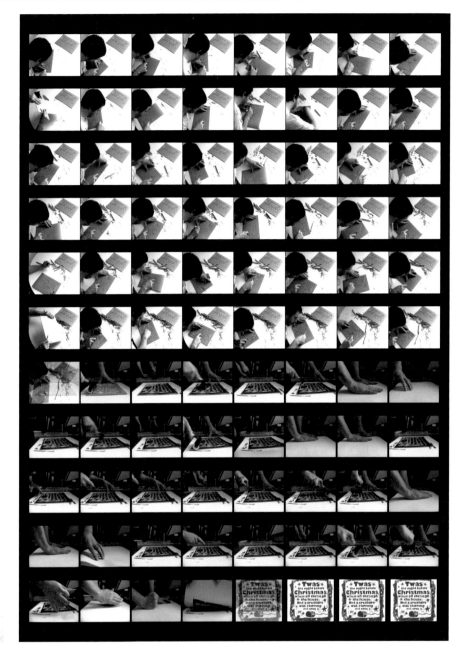

Christine Celic Strohl & Eric Strohl ✎

TDC NUMBERS POSTER • 2009 • POSTER *(top left & bottom)*
CLIENT Type Directors Club PRINTER Self-printed PRINTING Linocut
This two-color, hand-carved and hand-printed linocut was a part of the Type Directors Club of NYC invitational poster auction. The theme revolved around the economic crisis, primarily in regards to money and numbers. The final poster was printed on chipboard by hand-burnishing without the assistance of a press.

Chris Thornley ✎

NOT EVEN A MOUSE • 2008 • CHRISTMAS CARD *(top right)*
CLIENT Personal PRINTER Naylors PRINTING Linocut
Linocut study.

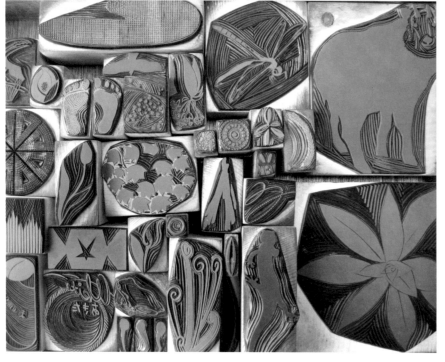

Tomoko Kataoka ↝

AFTER RAIN ARITHMETICS · 2006 · CARVED RUBBERPLATES *(top)*
CLIENT Personal PRINTER Self-printed PRINTING Rubber-print

UNTITLED · 2008 · LEAFLET *(left)*
CLIENT Yamada Shigeo Landscaping PRINTER Self-printed PRINTING Rubber-print

KIRIGAMI STAMPS · 2008 · CARVED ERASERS *(bottom)*
CLIENT Personal PRINTER Self-printed PRINTING Rubber-print

Tomoko Kataoka ◞

UNTITLED · 2004 · POSTCARD / CARVED ERASERS *(top, bottom)*
CLIENT Personal PRINTER Self-printed PRINTING Rubber-print

UNTITLED · 2005 · CARVED ERASERS *(middle, 2 images)*
CLIENT Personal PRINTER Self-printed PRINTING Rubber-print

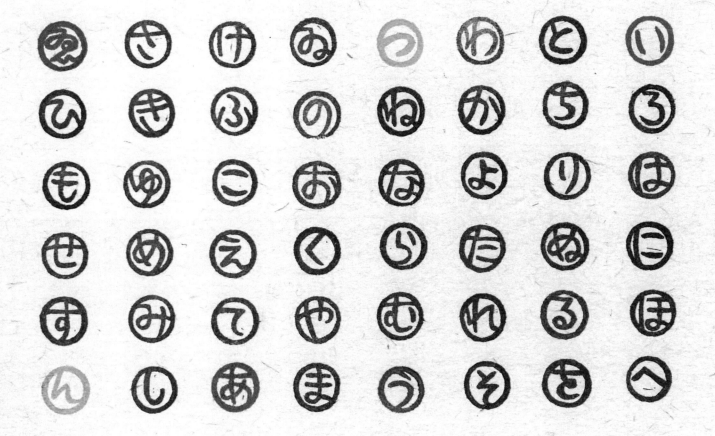

Jing Wei ✎

SLUG · 2008 · ART PRINT *(top left)*
MUSK OX · 2008 · ART PRINT *(top right)*
TURKEY · 2008 · ART PRINT *(bottom left)*
LLAMA · 2008 · ART PRINT *(bottom right)*
CLIENT The Believer PRINTER Self-printed PRINTING Woodblock print

BLOOD & THUNDER

"Upon the very cusp of theyr demonic deliuerance, arriueth a boatload of assholes."

Specious Speckled Lyre

Great Lugubrious Excuses

Cannonball Press ⌁

BLOOD AND THUNDER · 2008 · POSTER *(top left)*
SPECIOUS SPECKLED LYRE · 2009 · POSTER *(top middle)*
GREAT LUGUBRIOUS EXCUSES · 2009 · POSTER *(top right)*
SCARLET FACED CRAPPER · 2009 · POSTER *(bottom left)*
COMMON NAGGING REGRETS · 2009 · POSTER *(bottom right)*
CLIENT Personal PRINTER Self-printed PRINTING Letterpress - 1938 Vandercook No.24
DESIGNER *Martin Mazorra*

Scarlet Faced Crapper

Common Nagging Regrets

Tomoko Kataoka ∿

UNTITLED · 2004 · POSTCARDS *(3 images)*
CLIENT Underground book cafe PRINTER Self-printed PRINTING Rubber-print - Carved eraser

UNTITLED · 2005 · ART PRINT *(bottom right)*
CLIENT Personal PRINTER Self-printed PRINTING Rubber-print - Carved eraser

Marcus Walters

MOVE TO THE COUNTRY · 2007 · ART PRINT *(top left)*
NATURE TABLE · 2007 · ART PRINT *(top left)*
BIRDS · 2009 · ART PRINT *(top left)*
FLOWERS · 2009 · ART PRINT *(top left)*
CLIENT Personal PRINTER Get Casual Screenprinting PRINTING Screen-print

Landland ⋏

POSTER FOR BUILT TO SPILL · 2009 · POSTER *(top)*
CLIENT First Avenue PRINTER Landland PRINTING Screen-print
Four spot colors.
DESIGNER *Dan Black*

POSTER FOR MAGNOLIA ELECTRIC CO. · 2009 · POSTER *(bottom, 2 images)*
CLIENT Magnolia Electric Co. PRINTER Landland PRINTING Screen-print
DESIGN & TYPOGRAPHY *Dan Black* ILLUSTRATION *Jessica Seamans*

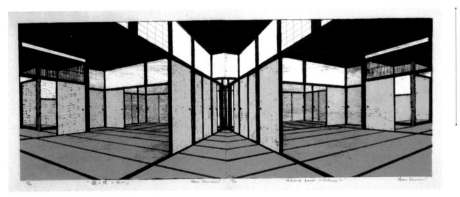

Nana Shiomi ◟

XXX · 2006 · ART PRINT
MIRROR ROOM - KATSURA · 2006 · ART PRINT
7TH MAY 1956, 8TH MAY 1956 · 2005 · ART PRINT
NEITHER CHERRY BLOSSOMS NOR AUTUMN LEAVES · 2007 · ART PRINT
CLIENT Personal PRINTER Baren PRINTING Woodcut print
Each an edition of 30.

Kenji Takenaka | Takezasado ▴

AO-SANJYO · 2002 · ART PRINT *(top)*
AKA-KIYOMIZU · 2003 · ART PRINT *(right)*
PINEAPPLE · 2006 · ART PRINT *(bottom)*
CLIENT Personal PRINTER Self-printed PRINTING Woodcut print

Natsuko Katahira ⌁

THE THING REMEMBERED UNTIL YESTERDAY · 2009 · JAPANESE PAPER *(top left)*
THE WAY TO A FOREST 3 · 2009 · JAPANESE PAPER *(top right)*
IN THE PLACE · 2007 · JAPANESE PAPER *(bottom left)*
THE WAY TO A FOREST · 2007 · JAPANESE PAPER *(bottom right)*
CLIENT Personal PRINTER Self-printed PRINTING Woodcut print

Yuki

ANNA · 2009 · LIMITED PRINT *(left page)*
CLIENT Personal PPRINTER Yuko Chikazawa PRINTING Woodcut print
"Eine einmalige Gelegenheit" collection, Berlin 2009

UTE KNEISEL · 2009 · ART PRINT *(top left)*
CRISTINA CAPUCHINA · 2009 · ART PRINT *(top right)*
VIOLA BINACCHI · 2009 · ART PRINT *(bottom left)*
BARBARA · 2009 · ART PRINT *(bottom middle)*
ANNETTE KÖHN · 2009 · ART PRINT *(bottom right)*
CLIENT Personal PRINTER Yuko Chikazawa PRINTING Woodcut print
"Portraits of our friends" collection, Berlin 2009

DESIGN + KONZEPT (ALL) *Maki Shimizu* WOODBLOCK CARVING + PRINTING (ALL) *Yuko Chikazawa*

2/16   春眠   2009/4/1

Camellia Finch ✿

SLEEP IN SPRING · 2009 · ART PRINT *(left page)*
CLIENT Personal PRINTER Self-printed PRINTING Printed by hand with ink and cardboard plate

U ✿

UNTITLED · 2009 · ART PRINT *(top left)*
CLIENT Personal PRINTER Self-printed PRINTING Woodcut print
The part of the flower acquires a color by Photoshop.

UNTITLED · 2008 · ART PRINT *(top right)*
CLIENT Personal PRINTER Self-printed PRINTING Woodcut print

LIGHT AND SHADE · 2008 · ART PRINT *(bottom right)*
CLIENT Personal PRINTER Self-printed PRINTING Woodcut print

Mocchi Mocchi ᴧ

JOURNEY INTO THE DISTANCE · 2008 · ART PRINT *(top left)*
CLIENT The Art Group PRINTER Self-printed PRINTING Screen-print

UNTITLED · 2009 · ART PRINT *(bottom left)*
DEER · 2009 · ART PRINT *(top right)*
FLOWER · 2009 · ART PRINT *(middle right)*
BLUEBIRD · 2009 · ART PRINT *(bottom right)*
CLIENT Personal PRINTER Self-printed PRINTING Screen-print

FLOWERS BLOSSOMING · 2008 · ART PRINT
CLIENT The Art Group PRINTER Self-printed PRINTING Screen-print

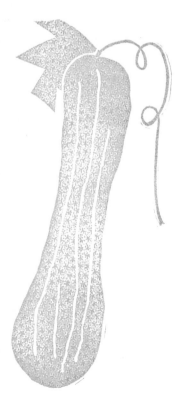

Tomoko Kataoka

NEW YEAR · 2009 · GREETING CARD *(top)*
UNTITLED · 2004 · ART PRINT *(bottom left)*
A LOOFAH · 2006 · ART PRINT *(bottom middle)*
NEW YEAR · 2005 · GREETING CARD *(bottom right)*
CLIENT Personal PRINTER Self-printed PRINTING Rubber-print · Carved eraser

Tomoko Kataoka ❧

UNTITLED · 2006 · EX LIBRIS *(top, 2 images)*
UNTITLED · 2005 · POSTCARD *(bottom left)*
UNTITLED · 2005 · EX LIBRIS *(bottom right)*
CLIENT Personal PRINTER Self-printed PRINTING Rubber-print - Carved eraser

Glossary •/•

Adana - British printing press manufacturer for small letterpress machines that can be moved and operated by hand. Between 1922 and 1999 many models were made, with the Adana 8x5 and the Adana 5x3 among the most popular.

Alugraphy - The missing link between classic lithography and modern ···> *offset printing*, using aluminium plates instead of stone ···> *lithography*. In opposite to classic lithography, the aluminium plate makes it possible to produce more prints from one original form. Mainly used for art prints.

Cast type ···> *Typeset*.

Chandler & Price - American printing press manufacturer, producing a wide range of letterpress printing machines from 1881 to 1964. ···> EXAMPLES: *Chandler & Price 12x18, Chandler & Price pilot, Chandler & Price Oldstyle Platen, Charles Brand Etching Press.*

Copperplate print - Actually the opposite of letterpress printing. The image is engraved into a copperplate. The ink fills the engraving, so–unlike letterpress printing–the surface stays clean. Therefore it is possible to print very fine structures (this was used printing bank notes).

Debossing - While ···> *embossing* raises the surfaces of materials, debossing works in reverse by pushing the surfaces of materials inward.

Die-cut - A die is a tool with a certain customized shape to cut exactly this shape out of a material (here: the printing paper). Die-cut means the decorative process itself. *Laser die-cut* does not use a customized tool, but cuts the shapes using a computer-controlled laser.

Embossing - Embossing raises surfaces (here: of paper) by using a die and counter die ···> *Die-cut*. It is used as a decorative technique to accent certain parts of a print. If used without ink, it is called *blind embossing*. Often combined with ···> *foil stamping*, which is called *hot foil embossing*.

Flatbed press - In general a printing press with a flat printing surface. The paper is either pressed against this surface by another flat plate (···> *Platen press)* or by a cylinder (···> *Proofing and Cylinder Presses*) rolling over it. ···> EXAMPLES: *Cincinatti flatbed press, FAG Control 405 flatbed cylinder proof press.* ···> SEE ALSO: *Rotary press.*

Foil stamping - Foil stamping is the application of pigment or foil (i.e. clear, colored or metallic foil) to paper where a heated die is stamped onto the foil, making it adhere to the surface and leaving the design of the die on the paper.

Gocco (print) - Gocco is a compact color screen-printing system (including an exposing device) for formats not bigger than approx. 15 x 20 cm. It was sold in Japan from 1977 to 2005. Gocco became immensely popular in Japan and it is estimated that one-third of Japanese households own a Gocco print system.

Hand press - The simplest form of a letterpress machine. Printing surface and paper sheet are pressed onto each other by either pressing them manually through two rubber cylinders or by pressing two plates together using a screw or a knuckle and lever. ···> EXAMPLES: *Albion press, Master printer sign press.*

Heidelberg - German printing press manufacturer, now specialized in offset presses, that gained notority in the mid-20th century with its letterpress machines like the famous "Heidelberger Tiegel", that was built until 1985. ···> EXAMPLES: *Heidelberg Windmill 10x15 = Original Heidelberg Automatic Platen Press.*

Hot type - Type casts (single embossed letterforms) made of molten metal (preferably lead) injected into negative letterforms, for the use in letterpress printing. ···> *Typesetting.*

Lead type ···> *Hot type, Typeset.*

Letterpress print - Letterpress printing is the oldest form of mechanical print reproduction. It is relief printing of text and image, in which a reversed, raised surface is inked and then pressed into a sheet of paper to obtain a positive right-reading image. There are a wide variety of printing presses and various forms of print templates, but all are based on the same principle.

Linocut / Linoprint - Linocut is a variant of woodcut in which a sheet of linoleum or linoleum-like material is used for the relief surface. A design is cut into the linoleum sheet, then inked with a roller, and finally impressed onto paper or fabric. The actual printing can be done by hand or with a press.

Lithography - Originally using stone with a completely smooth surface, nowadays anodized aluminium plates are used. The image is transfered by polymer applied to the surface. The smooth surface is divided into hydrophilic regions that reject ink, and hydrophobic (water repelling) regions that accept ink. Lithography lead to ···> *offset print.*

Magnesium plate - Etched magnesium plates are used for foil stamping, embossing, and debossing. A photosensitive coating applied to a special magnesium photo engraving plate allows the user to chemically etch an image into the magnesium plate after exposing a film negative and developing that image on the plate.

Metal type ···> *Hot type, Typeset.*

Offset print - In offset printing the inked image is transferred (or offset) from a plate to a rubber blanket, then to the printing surface. Offset printing is one of the most common printing techniques for bigger print runs today. Rather complex, it is not suitable for experimental techniques or (because of the cost involved) small print runs.

Platen press - Platen presses are powered by foot, steam, or electricity. Their main characteristic is that paper is fed into a "jaw" with the type on one side and paper on the other. Some have automatic feeds, so that paper does not have to be supplied by hand for each impression. ···> EXAMPLES: *Heidelberg Windmill 10x15 = Original Heidelberg Automatic Platen Press.*

Proofing and Cylinder presses - Presses using a cylinder to impress the paper on the form. Cylinder presses are characterized by using a large cylinder to deliver paper and impression to type on a flat bed. This principle is used by the latest letterpress machines (like the Heidelberg Cylinder machines) and precision proofing presses. ···> EXAMPLES: *1895 Poco proofing press, Stephenson Blake proofing press.*

Photopolymer - Photopolymer is a polymer that becomes solid when exposed to light, often in the ultraviolet spectrum. It is used to make printing templates for different types of print processes, as it is an easy, modern way to transfer an image onto the template.

Rotary press - In contrast to the flatbed press, the rotary press has a cylindrical printing surface. By rotation the printing surface is rolled over the paper, allowing much higher printing speed than flatbed presses.

Rubbercut, rubber-print - Rubbercuts are relief prints made by cutting silicone sheets. They work like woodblock print and linocut, apart from the different surface quality and therefore different print result.

Screen-print, Silkscreen print - Screen-printing is a printing technique that uses a woven mesh to support an ink-blocking stenciled image. The stencil forms open areas of mesh that transfer ink in the form of the image onto the paper. A squeegee is moved across the screen stencil, pumping ink past the threads of the woven mesh in the open areas. Often done by hand (for smaller editions or to get certain individual printing effects), there are also automatic screen-printing machines ···> EXAMPLES: *American Tempo silkscreen press*

Serigraphy ···> *Screen print.*

Spot color - A spot color is any color generated by a non-standard offset ink–such as metallic, fluorescent, spot varnish, or custom hand-mixed inks.

Stamping - Most simple form of printing by using pieces of rubber that have an image/text carved, molded, laser engraved, or vulcanized into them. The flexibility of the rubber surface leads to good print results.

Stock - Printing paper.

Typeset - Typesetting is the composition of text by putting together preproduced type casts (single embossed letterforms) in order to get a text print form for (mainly) letterpress printing. The type casts can be made out of metal (most common: lead), wood, rubber, or other materials.

Vandercook (& Sons) - An American manufacturer of proof presses from 1909 to 1969. ···> EXAMPLES: *Vandercook #4, Vandercook SP15, Vandercook 320G hand proof press, Vandercook SP20, Vandercook #24, Vandercook #3, Vandercook Universal 1.*

Wood type - Single (mostly quite big) letters made out of wood to be combined to words for letterpress printing. Well known are American wood types from the 19th century in a variety of fonts, often recognized by their bold Wild West design style.

Woodblock print, Woodcut print - The image is cut into an even block of wood in a way that the areas to show "white" are cut away with a knife, chisel, or sandpaper, leaving the characters or image to show in "black" at the original surface level. The ink is transferred from this remaining surface to the material. For color printing, multiple blocks are used, each for one colour, although overprinting two colours may produce further colours on the print. The wooden structures that are transfered to the final print are characteristic of this style of printing.

Contributors Index ⁙

Impressive ❧

PRINTMAKING, LETTERPRESS AND GRAPHIC DESIGN

EDITED BY Robert Klanten and Hendrik Hellige

ART DIRECTION & LAYOUT: Hendrik Hellige for Gestalten

PROJECT MANAGEMENT: Elisabeth Honerla for Gestalten

PRODUCTION MANAGEMENT: Janni Milstrey for Gestalten

PREFACE & INTERVIEWS: Sonja Commentz

PROOFREADING: English Express

TYPEFACE: Bonesana by Matthieu Cortat | FOUNDRY: www.gestalten.com/fonts

PRINTED BY Optimal Media Production, Röbel • Made in Germany

PUBLISHED BY Gestalten, Berlin 2010

ISBN: 978-3-89955-288-1

Respect copyrights, encourage creativity!

For more information, please check www.gestalten.com

Bibliographic information published by the Deutsche Nationalbibliothek. The Deutsche Nationalbibliothek lists this publication in the Deutsche Nationalbibliografie; detailed bibliographic data is available on the internet at http://dnb.d-nb.de.

None of the content in this book was published in exchange for payment by commercial parties or designers; Gestalten selected all included work based solely on its artistic merit.

This book has been printed on FSC certified paper which ensures responsible paper sources with sustainable forest management.

Gestalten is a climate neutral company and so are our products. We collaborate with the non-profit carbon offset provider myclimate (www.myclimate.org) to neutralize the company's carbon footprint produced through our worldwide business activities by investing in projects that reduce CO_2 emissions (www.gestalten.com/myclimate).